EDWARD ELGAR

CLASSIC *f*M LIFELINES

EDWARD ELGAR

AN ESSENTIAL GUIDE TO HIS LIFE AND WORKS

DAVID NICE

PAVILION

First published in Great Britain in 1996 by
PAVILION BOOKS LIMITED
26 Upper Ground, London SE1 9PD

Copyright © Pavilion Books Ltd 1996
Front cover illustration © The Hulton Deutsch Collection 1996

Edited and designed by Castle House Press, Llantrisant, South Wales
Cover designed by Bet Ayer

A CIP catalogue record for this book is available
from the British Library

ISBN 1 85793 977 8

Set in Lydian and Caslon
Printed and bound in Great Britain by Mackays of Chatham

2 4 6 8 10 9 7 5 3 1

This book can be ordered direct from the publisher.
Please contact the Marketing Department.
But try your bookshop first.

Contents

ACKNOWLEDGMENTS

For Trude

Special thanks are due to Andrew Neill of the Elgar Society, for help and conversations surrounding two lectures to its knowledgeable members; to the curator of the Elgar Birthplace Museum, Broadheath, for allowing me to spend a peaceful afternoon studying the sketches of the *Second Symphony* several years ago; to the residents of various Elgar sites around Malvern, for tolerating my party of Summer School visitors; and to Jeremy, as ever.

A NOTE FROM THE EDITORS

A biography of this type inevitably contains numerous references to pieces of music. The paragraphs are also peppered with 'quotation marks', since much of the tale is told through reported speech.

Because of this, and to make things more accessible for the reader as well as easier on the eye, we decided to simplify the method of typesetting the names of musical works. Conventionally this is determined by the nature of the individual work, following a set of rules whereby some pieces appear in italics, some in italics and quotation marks, others in plain roman type and others still in roman and quotation marks.

In this book, the names of all musical works are simply set in italics. Songs and arias appear in italics and quotation marks.

CHAPTER I

MUSIC IN THE AIR
(1857–88)

- ◆ *Worcestershire childhood*
- ◆ *Youthful inspirations*
- ◆ *The Three Choirs Festival*
- ◆ *Violinist of promise*
- ◆ *First performances*

At the height of his creative inspiration in July 1900, the 43-year-old Edward Elgar wrote to his friend and adviser A.J. Jaeger from Birchwood, his summer retreat at the north end of the Malvern Hills: 'The trees are singing my music – or have I sung theirs? I suppose I have.' For Elgar, the supposition was really a certainty. Music had always been in the air of his native Worcestershire, written on the wind or carried along the streams and rivers where he had spent many a reflective childhood hour. In characteristically nostalgic, retrospective mood, he confided to a friend in 1921 that he was 'still at heart the dreamy child who used to be found in the reeds by Severn side with a sheet of paper, trying to fix the sounds & longing for something very great – source, texture and all else unknown.'

He was born on 2 June 1857 at Broadheath, humbly located between the river Severn, which flowed past the city of Worcester and the forested slopes of Birchwood. The group of 'Scotch firs' near the small cottage, now a charmingly tended museum and archive with a well-kept garden, played an important part in his imagination: if not consciously from infancy – he was only two when the family moved to Worcester – then from return visits in childhood. 'I can smell them now,' he told a friend visiting Broadheath in 1920.

His attitude to the human scene, the family and friends, of his childhood seems to have been more ambivalent. The conclusion to that often-quoted self-portrait of the Severn-side boy sounds a typically excessive note of self-pity: 'as a child . . . no single person was ever kind to me.' It stems partly, and perhaps understandably given the circumstances of the time, from a sense of inferiority at being the struggling son of a man 'in trade', a social position of which he was to be reminded later in life as the husband of a major general's daughter. Yet his father's trade was a musical one, and if he did not give any active encouragement to the young Edward's talents in that direction, there was never a sense of parental disapproval or unmusical indifference to bar the way.

William Henry Elgar from Dover – the surname, of Saxon origin, means 'fairy-spear' – came to Worcestershire on the recommendation of the London music publishers to whom he had been apprenticed, Coventry and Hollier of Dean Street, to tune pianos at Witley Court for Queen Adelaide, widow of William IV. The royal connection brought him more work as a piano tuner, although he took his discipline at leisure, travelling to his places of 'work' in an unorthodox way. 'There is a touch of fantasy,' wrote Elgar's first major biographer, Basil Maine, 'about this small, spare man of delicate features riding a thoroughbred horse in order to keep an appointment to tune a piano. It is difficult to imagine a man who could make so extravagant a gesture, sitting down to conquer a column of figures in a ledger.'

Unfortunately, that was what William Elgar found himself called upon to do when, joining forces with his younger brother, he extended the piano-tuning business to a shop selling sheet music in Worcester High Street. After settling briefly at several addresses in the town, the family was eventually compelled to move to rooms above the shop when Edward was six (all that now remains of shop and lodgings, in the centre of the nightmare of 1960s town redevelopment that is Worcester today, is a plaque on a modern building near the Cathedral).

The father's real passions lay elsewhere. As a violinist, he played for the genial weekly meetings of the Worcester Glee Club at the Crown Hotel and – more significantly – among the second violins when the Three Choirs Festival, shared in yearly rotation between Worcester, Hereford and Gloucester, came to town. Young Edward, encouraged in violin lessons from an early age, would join him and, playing out the all-too-familiar pattern of father–son rivalry, even supersede him in both organizations.

William Elgar also had another, rather surprising commitment. Since 1846, he had been the organist of St George's, where his duties, reluctantly and often haphazardly undertaken, included original composition and training the choir. The church was a Catholic haven in the English cathedral city, and William a lifelong Protestant; but his position led to a bizarre, if latent conflict of family interests. In 1848 he had married Ann Greening, 'descended', according to Elgar's amendment of a biographical note in 1900, 'from the fine, old *yeoman* stock of Weston, Herefordshire – therefore intensely English.' Following her husband to St George's to keep him company, she became intensely Catholic, too, converting to the faith in 1852. The irascible William never approved, but could only threaten; someone who came to know the family well later commented: 'old man a regular terror as regards the Catholicity of his family – used to threaten to shoot his daughters if caught going to confession.'

Ann Elgar's conversion was the typically single-minded action of a strong and ardent woman. There can be no doubt that Edward loved her dearly. She communicated to him something of her intense feeling for nature – the Blakean ability 'to see a World in a Grain of Sand / And a Heaven in a Wild Flower' – and her conviction that one must 'be always busy, doing something that is useful and interesting.' Prone to verse-making of her own, she was well read, and the enthusiasm for Longfellow she shared with her son was to bear fruit in the 1890s with his cantatas *The Black Knight* and *Scenes from the Saga of King Olaf*. He would look back on *Hyperion* as the book 'from which I, as a child, received my first idea of the great German nations', and listed among other formative influences in his reading other works which, like Longfellow's, have ceased to be standard fare today: Sir Philip Sydney's *Arcadia*, Baker's Chronicles and Drayton's *Polyalbion*.

The tenacity of Edward's mother in her intellectual pursuits seems all the more remarkable given the constant demands of her seven children. Only Edward was Broadheath-born; his three elder siblings, Harry, Lucy and Pollie (Susannah Mary), had been born – as Lucy later put it – 'within the shadow of our dear, old cathedral.' It was the impending birth of a fifth child, Jo, that necessitated the move back to the city from Ann's beloved countryside. The two youngest children were Frank, who followed Edward's musical ambition after his own more modest fashion, and Dot, who became a nun. Dot's health as a baby seemed the most fragile, but only a few months after her birth the spectre of premature mortality, which haunted many a Victorian household, claimed the fifteen-year-old Harry as its first victim. Delicate Jo, nicknamed 'young Beethoven' and destined in his parents' eyes to be the real musical genius of the family, died two years later of scarlet fever at the age of seven. The vivid realization of sickness and death in *The Dream of Gerontius* has its roots in Elgar's childhood intimations of mortality. Father Waterworth of St George's hoped to console young Edward with an engraving of St Joseph, calmly awaiting his end. The words on the back of the picture included the line 'Jesus, Mary, Joseph, pray for me in my own agony' – taken from the (then) recently published *Dream of Gerontius* by Father Newman of Birmingham. When setting the poem over thirty years later, Elgar well remembered the prayer, and the circumstances under which he first saw it.

Young Edward's susceptibility to feminine influence was compounded by his first steps in education – at a Catholic 'Dame's school' wearing 'petticoats & with his sisters & other girls', as the son of a friend recalled. His next school at Spetchley Park furnishes an image of the boy gazing out of the classroom window at the great trees in the park swaying in the wind. At the point in *The Dream of Gerontius* when the Soul reaches the House of Judgment, he hears music 'like the rushing of the wind – / The summer wind among the lofty pines'; and sure enough, it was in the Spetchley library copy of the score that Elgar in old age sanctified another memory, inscribing alongside the passage 'In Spetchley Park'. After Spetchley, he moved on to Littleton House. Here, too, were seeds to bear future fruit: he never forgot one remark of Littleton's much-respected schoolmaster, Francis Reeve: 'the Apostles were poor men, young men at the time of their calling; perhaps before the descent of the Holy Ghost not cleverer than some of you here.' That was the basis of *The Apostles* in 1903.

Littleton's most profound significance for Edward, though, was that it lay – as he later put it – 'to the brightly-lit west' of the city, entailing a ferry journey (to 'the Broadheath side') across the beloved Severn. Ann Elgar asked thirteen-year-old Hubert Leicester, the nephew of a family friend, to accompany him –

initiating a friendship that lasted a lifetime. In 1932, Elgar remembered how the sun at their backs on the morning ferry-journey ' "shot vital gold", filling Payne's Meadows with glory and illuminating for two small boys a world to conquer and to love.' Hubert gives us one of three concurring portraits of Elgar around this time: 'a most miserable-looking lad – legs like drumsticks – with nothing of a boy about him', although it should be added that Edward had already developed a lifelong love of 'japes', wordplay and miscellaneous high jinks, while Hubert was the serious, studious one. Schoolmaster Reeve recalled that Elgar 'did not attract much attention. He was very shy and reserved, and was considered rather delicate; he had no taste for the rough games and rarely joined in them.' Ann Elgar, writing couplets on all her children in 1874, described Edward as:

> *Nervous, sensitive and kind,*
> *Displays no vulgar frame of mind.*

Sensitivity and kindness found some outlet in his first musical exercises. A summer holiday in Broadheath at the age of ten prompted the jotting of a lively melody, a jig of the sort familiar since Handel's day, in 12/8 time. When he came to write music for a play, to be enacted by the Elgar children in front of their parents, he used the 'tune from Broadheath' for a scene featuring 'Fairies and Giants' (the giants cavorting to a distorted version not far removed from the *Dies irae* or Latin chant for the dead, familiar perhaps from visits to St George's). The conflict of the play – to be developed by J.M. Barrie and (most significantly for Elgar in 1915) Algernon Blackwood – was between childhood imagination and adult incomprehension: the Two Old People in the drama, lured into the magic world beyond the stream, failed to respond to magic and had to be charmed to sleep.

When Elgar re-employed many of his earlier inspirations in the two *Wand of Youth* Suites in 1907, two of the old stage directions remained, somewhat enigmatically in that context. An 'old-style' Minuet reads 'Andante. (The two old people enter)', while in Suite One, No.Five, 'two fairy pipers enter in a boat and charm them to sleep.' In the 'Slumber Scene' that follows, the bass consists of only three notes – all that could be managed by the child playing the original instrument, a home-made affair requiring three pounds of nails. Orchestral means at the time were, of course, limited; but in 1907 Elgar was able to engage a full orchestra with consummate skill. He thought of the pieces as mere trifles, but many of the themes, especially at the heart of 'Fairy Pipers' and 'The Little Bells', capture the introspective essence of the private Elgar as movingly as anything in his larger-scale works.

The play was never staged, and Elgar's own 'Wand of Youth' came to a premature end when, at the age of fifteen, he left Littleton House and went to work in the office of a Worcester solicitor, William Allen. Whether he made the decision as a result of parental pressure, or because he felt obliged to help the family's precarious finances, we do not know; but a year later he was free, having learnt enough of legal jargon to poke fun at it but little of legal practices. In this respect he was luckier than Tchaikovsky, whose legal education at the instigation of a well-meaning but unmusical father led to several years of misery as a clerical officer.

He had hoped to go to Leipzig to receive the kind of musical education attained by Britain's leading composers at the time, Charles Villiers Stanford and Arthur Sullivan; now he had to be content with self-help. Assisting in his father's shop, he had access to the scores of Mozart's Masses and Beethoven's symphonies in the popular piano-duet arrangements of the time (in 1873 he incorporated themes from the symphonies he knew in a *Credo* for St George's, under the pseudonym 'Bernard Pappenheim'). In 1904 he would be able to declare himself 'self-taught in the matter of harmony, counterpoint, form, and, in short, the whole of the "mystery" of music'; chief among his guides were Catel's *Treatise on Harmony*, Cherubini's *Counterpoint* and an English translation of the so-called (and apparently unauthentic) *Mozart's Thorough-bass school*, which he was to look back on as 'the first real sort of friendly leading I had. . . . There was something in that to go upon, something human.'

Organ handbooks helped him to lessen his father's workload at St George's, although his real education in the organ and church-anthem repertoire came from visits to the 'other side' at the cathedral. The inauguration of a new cathedral organ brought a host of distinguished visitors, including Samuel Sebastian Wesley, grandson of the hymnwriter Charles Wesley and, like his father (plain Samuel) a composer. Elgar was full of admiration for Samuel Sebastian's series of large-scale anthems, published in 1853, but on this occasion he was impressed by the way Wesley the organist 'built up a wonderful climax of sound before crashing into the subject of the "*Wedge*" [E minor] *Fugue* of Bach'.

It was at the cathedral, too, that the organist William Done, so conservative in his tastes that he found the music of Schumann 'preposterous', kept the flame of earlier English church music burning. So Elgar was at least made aware of the legacy before Purcell, Britain's greatest native-born composer – even if he did regard the music of Byrd, Orlando Gibbons and Tallis, as he told his biographer Basil Maine, 'interesting . . . merely as museum specimens.' His own early exercises in choral writing for St George's are modest and intimate in scale, quite without the vulgarity of much Catholic church music composed at the time: the first setting of '*O salutaris hostia*' and '*Tantum ergo*' look forward to the mature Elgar in the flexibility of line. So, too, does the '*Ave Maria*' of 1887, by which time – with William Elgar ousted by the dogmatic younger Catholics in the church, and his successor gone – he took over what had once been his father's post and hated it ('the choir is awful & no good to be done with them').

The earlier days at St George's were more carefree. He gave Hubert Leicester his first taste of Wagner, a composer he told Hubert was 'not understood . . . you will hear more of him some day,' by playing the Overture to *Tannhäuser* as an organ voluntary. In the more relaxed atmosphere of the Glee Club, where his piano accompaniments, skilfully adjusted for wayward singers, were much in demand, he arranged the Overture to *The Flying Dutchman* for the odd assortment of instruments available. His father, who had been responsible for Glee Club arrangements of his own, looked on warily. He was also spending the half-hour or more of sermons at St George's up in the organ loft writing out music for wind quintet.

In the summer of 1877, he had been engaged as 'efficient Leader and Instructor' of the newly formed Worcester Amateur Instrumental Society, and in addition to his violinistic skills he now mastered the bassoon. It came in very useful for one particular splinter-group from the society, a small wind group whose other members were Hubert Leicester and his younger brother Willie, Frank Exton and Edward's younger brother Frank.

It was hardly a wind quintet as most composers knew it – there were two flutes (Hubert and Exton) rather than the usual one and no horn – and while Frank was an oboist of distinction, Willie's clarinet expertise was rather below the level of the rest, so Elgar's writing for that instrument had to play safe. Nevertheless the results, fairly recently unearthed, do the young composer credit. The Six *Promenades* reveal both wit and concision: in the Andante titled 'Somniferous', Elgar distributes the theme neatly between the five instruments before giving himself (on bassoon) the gruff last word, while the ensuing *Allegro molto* has a graciousness worthy of Richard Strauss, who in his late years returned to the form of the wind serenade in homage to Mozart. It is Mozart whose spirit lies somewhat obviously behind the series of '*Harmony Music*' (or 'Shed' Music, after the cramped place of rehearsal). No.4 is Elgar's earliest piece of music on a large scale, with its rhythmically lively farmyard sounds and a brace of fine melodic ideas flowing easily into each other (one is clearly related to the second theme of Beethoven's overture to *Coriolan*). Even so, the elliptical *Intermezzos* of 1879 are the most original of the wind quintet pieces, as Elgar acknowledged when he singled them out as 'mine own children.'

More light music was composed as the result of a once-a-week appointment. The governors of Powick County Lunatic Asylum were forward-looking enough to realize that music could only have a beneficial effect upon the patients. So Elgar's commission was to rehearse a motley band of musically-inclined attendants at the asylum. His sad reflection that 'I fear my tunes did little to ameliorate the condition of the unfortunate inmates' might not be shared by most musicians working in music therapy today; but perhaps the form of the quadrille, first a military and later a ballroom dance to be executed by the dancers in elaborate patterns, should not have been the exclusive form of therapy recommended by the hospital administration. At any rate, the experience could only have been grist to the mill of Elgar's music experience in the round and he found himself able to draw on some of the quadrille themes in works to come.

If Powick must have seemed like a step back into the merely provincial daily round, there was always Worcester's triennial role in the Three Choirs Festival to remind Elgar of the world beyond. Since its inauguration in 1724, the Three Choirs Festival had expanded from its modest origins as a showcase for the cathedral choir and organ, to embrace neighbouring choral societies, an ever-increasing orchestra consisting mostly of local musicians, and visiting solo artists from the great metropolis. The bastions of its programing were the only two oratorios before *The Dream of Gerontius* to stand the test of time – and neither were by English-born composers. To open the festival there was Mendelssohn's *Elijah*, crowning glory of the composer's long association with Britain and conducted by him at its Birmingham Festival premiere in 1846. A measure of its popularity can be gathered from a letter Elgar wrote in 1903 encouraging an analysis of *The Apostles* and pointing out that '*Elijah* we have heard dissected ever since our babyhood.' He may not have cared to emulate its more placid aspect, of which the finest representatives are the bass aria '*Lord God of Abraham*' and the contralto number '*O rest in the Lord* '. Yet he took to heart Mendelssohn's use of recurring themes to strengthen the dramatic backbone of the Biblical tale long before he knew the operas of Wagner in their entirety.

As for Handel's *Messiah*, which usually provided the final flourish of the Festival, Elgar came to know it by significant degrees. At the 1866 Festival, an orchestral rehearsal of '*O thou that tellest good tidings to Zion*' prompted him to go home and try the tune out on the violin with the aid of an instruction manual: his first violin lesson, self-taught. In 1869 the Elgar Brothers' firm supplied the orchestral parts for *Messiah*, and Edward managed to insert a theme of his own into the score. It reached performance, much to William Elgar's fury.

Between *Elijah* at the beginning of the festival and *Messiah* at its close came a desert of undistinguished works. In a perceptive and candid memoir of the composer she came to know so well, Rosa Burley neatly summarizes:

> *New music was certainly produced but it was chosen by very conservative standards, and for every* Messiah *or* Elijah *discovered, there were countless cantatas on Biblical subjects by cathedral organists, teachers of harmony and other not very highly inspired professional musicians, which, having been sung once, were thankfully dropped for ever. It was said that nearly every line of the Bible was ultimately used for some cantata or other – except of course the genealogical tables.*

During the 1880s, there were two notable exceptions to the rule. One was the 1884 visit of Antonin Dvořák, who conducted a sacred work, his *Stabat Mater*, and a secular one, the *Sixth Symphony*. Elgar, now among the first violins, was captivated. He wrote to a newly acquired friend, the Yorkshire doctor and cellist Charles William Buck, whom he had met while playing for a British Medical Association convention in Worcester, 'I wish you could hear Dvořák's music. It is simply ravishing, so tuneful & clever & the orchestration is wonderful; no matter how few instruments he uses it never sounds thin.' The sunny themes of Dvořák's most wholesomely flowing symphony must have beguiled him, too; if the slow movement can fairly be called the happiest of its kind in nineteenth-century symphonic literature, then Elgar was to find an even greater serenity in the Adagio of his own *First Symphony*.

He absorbed little of Hubert Parry's *Scenes from Shelley's Prometheus Unbound*, although at the 1886 Three Choirs Festival held in Gloucester, it seemed like a breath of fresh air. Neither the work itself nor one critic's enthusiastic claim that English music had at last come into its own with a masterpiece bear close scrutiny now, although Parry was to go on to greater things with his resplendent choral ode *Blest Pair of Sirens*, the stirring coronation anthem of 1902 *I Was Glad* and the famous melody of '*Jerusalem*' (which Elgar orchestrated in 1922).

Elgar's objection was to Parry's sense of orchestration, which he found 'dead & never more than an *organ part arranged*' (a view he contradicted, however, in later life). Although Parry was frequently ready to lend him a helping hand, he would bracket him resentfully with the lesser creative spirits of Charles Villiers Stanford – a frequent target of unkind fun on Elgar's part – and Alexander Mackenzie as part of the academic musical establishment (although in 1881 he had welcomed Mackenzie's cantata *The Bride* in much the same terms as the critic hailed Parry's *Prometheus Unbound*).

The finest tunesmith (and, within his own limits, orchestrator) was Arthur Sullivan, whose gift for setting words in a natural and memorable way Elgar never quite rivalled; but his talents were more fully engaged on the series of Savoy operettas with W.S. Gilbert than in the occasional cantata – of which *The Golden Legend*, which appeared in the same year, 1886, as *Prometheus*

Unbound, soon became a hoary favourite of the festival circuit.

The Three Choirs Festival was only part of Elgar's cultural initiation. Operas he came to know through playing the violin in the tiny pit orchestra for the visiting Haig-Dyer Opera Company, and his lifelong passion for Shakespeare was encouraged first by a burly assistant in his father's shop, Ned Spiers, who played out many a part before his eyes – from Macbeth to Caliban – and then, later, through the readings of the famous actress Mrs. Macready. Even such diverse experiences, however, were not sufficient for a young would-be composer whose real education was to hear as much new or recent music as possible, and London beckoned. He went there first in 1877 to study with the violinist Adolphe Pollitzer, whose training linked him, through two generations of teachers, to Beethoven. If funds would not run to study in Leipzig, £7 15s. 4d. could buy a train ticket to London and five lessons with Pollitzer.

His tutor told him he could make him one of the finest violinists in the country; but after several return visits over the next few years, he gave up for the very reason that had launched his determination in the first place: hearing the great virtuoso August Wilhelmj play. On the second occasion, in 1884, the strength of Wilhelmj's tone convinced him that his own would never be sufficiently powerful; and this time, when he asked Pollitzer: 'Shall I be first class?' the answer – 'You will be very good' – sealed his fate: he would pursue a career as a violinist no further than to teach and to complete the occasional salon piece (several of which, especially the *Idylle* of 1884, are useful additions to the repertoire).

Yet London still had so much to offer. In 1856, at the recently re-erected Crystal Palace in Sydenham, the musically-minded engineer George Grove and the conductor August Manns launched a series of Saturday popular concerts. To these Elgar came, and a year before his death in 1934 he re-lived the experience:

> *I rose at six, walked a mile to the railway station, the train left at seven; arrived at Paddington about 11, underground to Victoria, on to the Palace arriving in time for the last three-quarters of an hour of the rehearsal; if fortune smiled, this piece of rehearsal included the work desired to be heard; but fortune rarely smiled and more often than not the principal*

item was over. Lunch. Concert at three. At five a rush to Victoria; then to Paddington, on to Worcester arriving at 10.30. A strenuous day indeed: but the new work had been heard and another treasure added to a life's experience.

Among the works he heard were several by Berlioz, a perfect lesson in instrumentation. Of the three movements he heard Manns conduct from the *Symphonie fantastique*, the March to the Scaffold clearly made its mark, for he played it as an organ voluntary following a christening at St George's. When the father of the baptized asked 'the name of that beautiful tune you were playing,' he tactfully replied 'a march by a French composer.'

Crystal Palace was by no means the only place to hear great music. Only a year after conducting the 1880 world premiere of Wagner's *Der Ring des Nibelungen* at the composer's new festival theatre in Bayreuth, the Austro-Hungarian conductor Hans Richter guided a new series of concerts at the St James' Hall. His programme included not only Berlioz's exquisite, orchestrally refined song cycle *Les nuits d'été* ('Summer Nights') but also the Overture to Wagner's *Die Meistersinger von Nürnburg*. When Elgar heard the Prelude and Liebestod from *Tristan und Isolde* at a Crystal Palace concert commemorating Wagner's death in 1883 he wrote in his programme: 'This is the finest thing of W.'s that I have heard up to the present. I shall never forget this.'

His long-awaited trip to Germany was then fresh in his memory, although the music of Wagner played a relatively small part in the concerts he attended. This was not his first experience of foreign travel; he had accompanied his sister Lucy's fiancée Charlie Pipe to Paris in 1880. Then, they had heard Saint-Saëns play the organ at the Madeleine before enjoying the more ribald pleasures of café and music-hall (duly to find cheerful expression in a new set of Powick quadrilles). The Leipzig cultural fare centred around the venerable concert-hall institution of the Gewandhaus. Elgar told Charles Buck about some of the music he had heard in the Leipzig Gewandhaus that January: first Haydn's '*Surprise*' *Symphony* – 'strange to go so far to hear so little' – followed by healthy doses of 'Schumann (my ideal!), Brahms, Rubinstein & Wagner.' Schumann was Manns' ideal too, although for Elgar, Schumann's pride of place was to yield to Brahms when he heard Richter conduct Brahms's *Third Symphony* in London a year later. Today it seems strange that there should have then been division in the musical world between those who supported Brahms and the iconoclastic Wagnerians. Richter saw no reason, however, to favour the one at the expense of the other; nor did Elgar, who was to write eloquently on the (then) new *Third Symphony* in the *Malvern Advertiser* and was later (in 1905) to conduct and lecture on the symphony.

There was another 'ideal' involved in the trip to Germany: Helen Weaver, daughter of a Worcester shoe merchant, who was studying music there. Elgar and Helen spent most of the time in the company of her fellow student Edith Groveham, and there is little evidence to point to a romance. That summer, however, he wrote to Charles Buck 'The vacation at Leipzig begins shortly; my 'Braut' arrives on Thursday next . . . after [her departure] 'twould be a charity if you could find a broken-hearted fiddler much trio-playing for a day or two.'

So little is known about Elgar's relationship with Helen that even in 1968, when Michael Kennedy's sympathetic study of Elgar was published, it was assumed that the 'bride' in question, because of the German word employed, was herself of that nationality. However much food the unofficial and obscurely documented engagement may since have provided for trivial romancing, the relationship is remarkable both for its rarity – if Elgar had any time for love prior to meeting Helen, we know even less about it – and its brevity: Helen's stepmother died at the end of the year, and it may have been the uncertain prospect of marrying a penurious musican, and a Catholic to boot, that led her to break off the engagement. What we do know is that Elgar was miserable. In January 1884 he told Buck, 'I am disappointed, disheartened & sick of this world altogether' – a frequent complaint throughout his correspondence, although on this occasion he meant it. Hearing the news that Buck was himself to be married that summer, he revealed that 'things have not prospered with me this year at all, my prospects are worse than ever & to crown my miseries my engagement is broken off & I am lonely . . . I have not the heart to speak to anyone.'

Speculation suggests Helen Weaver, and not the previously-cited Lady Mary Lygon, as the person behind the mysterious asterisks of '*Enigma*'s thirteenth variation. At the time, though, it was Buck's Yorkshire hospitality that inspired significant musical thoughts. On his first visit to the doctor's village of Giggleswick, Elgar sketched music for a trio, to be played by himself, Charles in his capacity as cellist, and the doctor's mother as pianist. '*Douce pensée*', as he then called it, begins charmingly in a manner reminiscent of Sullivan at his most tender, but becomes more adventurous in its harmonies and then opens out onto a sequence of sinking regret before its skilful close. That sequence sounds an authentic note of the mature Elgar, as he acknowledged when, in 1915, he arranged the piece for small orchestra as *Rosemary – that's for remembrance*.

On another Yorkshire visit in the still-happy summer of the 'Leipzig year', Buck took him to Lake Windermere and witnessed a phenomenon: the dumbstruck composer began to 'write furiously' and then 'said he had never known quite the same sensation before.' The intended scale of the resulting *Lakes Overture* proved beyond his grasp. He did complete a *Scottish Overture* on a comparable scale, following a holiday in Scotland that included a brief romantic interlude with a girl referred to only as 'E.E.' (his own initials) – but the results were not encouraging. When he showed it to William Cole Stockley, chorus-master for the Birmingham Festival and enterprising conductor of a Popular Concerts series in that city, 'he candidly said he could not read the Score & it sounded to him disconnected.' It probably was; the solution to large-scale composition did not come to Elgar overnight.

Stockley had shown no hesitation, however, in giving the composer his first encouragement when it came to the musical genre of the polished trifle. A year after Elgar had taken his place among the first violins of the Birmingham orchestra, Stockley featured his *Intermezzo mauresque* in the programme of 13 December 1883. A critic described it as 'melodious, graceful and pleasing . . . the scoring . . . tasteful and musicianly.' All of which is true, at least in the form that we now know it: the outer portions of the *Sérénade mauresque*, Op.10 No.2, make the same graceful nod in the direction of Moorish music that we hear in *Anitra's Dance* from Grieg's incidental music to *Peer Gynt*, while the central section sounds a pastoral note closer to Elgar's own surroundings. A second piece with a fashionably Spanish title, *Sevillana*, was of a more obvious cut, featuring a series of felicitous waltz themes scored with a rumbustious touch that was to be better handled in *Cockaigne* and *In the South*. This time it was Manns, on the recommendation of Pollitzer, who included it in a Crystal Palace concert in May 1884 – Elgar's London debut as a composer.

Successful though *Sevillana* proved on that occasion, it was the *Intermezzo* that merited closer inspection. By 1888, it had become part of a four-movement Suite, premiered by Stockley's orchestra on 23 February with the composer conducting. Most of the Birmingham critics were 'nettled' since, Elgar wrote to Buck, 'I am the only local man who has been asked to conduct his own work – & what's a greater offence, I *did it* – and *well* too.'

The most distinguished of the *Intermezzo*'s three companions was a *Fantasia Gavotte*, based on an incident during the Leipzig visit: 'I saw two dancers . . . who came down the stage in antique dress dancing a Gavotte: when they reached the footlights they suddenly turned round and appeared to be two very young and modern people and danced a gay and lively measure.' The more distant origins of the piece would seem to be the music for the children's play: the Minuet of the Two Old People, interrupted by fairies and giants. At any rate, the whimsy is done with a delicious lightness of touch, possibly refined in the 1899 revision, which bears the title *Contrasts (The Gavotte, AD 1700 and 1900)*.

By July 1888 the 'Birmingham Suite' was 'ancient history', and Elgar proudly informed Buck of three movements for strings, which had just been performed by the Worcester Musical Union (very probably the prototypes for the masterly *Serenade for strings* of 1892). '*I like 'em* (The first thing I ever did),' he wrote. 'Also there's a terrific (!!!) song in this month's Maga[zine]: of Music.'

The text to the song, '*The Wind at Dawn*', was by Caroline Alice Roberts, a piano pupil of Elgar's since October 1886. The following year they were married.

CHAPTER 2
CHORUS AND ORCHESTRA
(1889–97)

- ♦ Alice
- ♦ Large-scale commissions
- ♦ Holidays in Bavaria
- ♦ The triumph of King Olaf
- ♦ Enter Jaeger

Caroline Alice Roberts was a major general's daughter. So, too, was Pauline de Ahna, the woman Elgar's greatest musical contemporary, Richard Strauss, would marry. Yet the differences in their respective families' reactions are striking. Major General de Ahna and his wife had enthused over the young Bavarian composer's prospects – for, unlike Elgar, he already had a modest success to his credit when he met the family in 1887, namely the tone-poem *Aus Italien*.

So Pauline was on her own when she petulantly attempted to pull rank in the many tempestuous moments of the Strausses' fundamentally loving marriage. This is vividly illustrated in the composer's beguiling autobiographical opera *Intermezzo*, where the wife declares: 'We know about your relations! Don't you dare compare them to my distinguished family!' By contrast, Alice's father, a knight commander of the British Empire in recognition of his distinguished career in the Indian Army, was no longer alive when she came to Elgar for lessons, and her mother died a year before their engagement in September 1887; but the relatives' response to the engagement was one of stern disapproval. One aunt even cut Alice out of her will.

Rosa Burley, headmistress of the school at which Elgar taught the violin, and soon to become a friend, recalled sitting in front of two upper-class ladies at the 1893 premiere of Elgar's *Spanish Serenade* and hearing their objections:

> *... dear old Lady Roberts of Redmarley ... would certainly not have allowed such a marriage had she been alive to prevent it. Friends of the family had simply not known what to do. They did not wish to cut Alice Roberts – though apparently a good many of them had done so – but they naturally felt that they could not be expected to meet a man whose father kept a wretched little shop in Worcester and even tuned their pianos. It was all most awkward.*

The response was typical of the rigid social distinctions still in place in Victorian England, and Gilbert and Sullivan were hardly exaggerating when they parodied it in their Savoy operas. Well might Elgar declare, along with Ralph Rackstraw in *HMS Pinafore* (1878), 'I love, and love, alas, above my station!' Infinitely less secure than Strauss, he was poorly constituted to take in his stride what slights he might encounter, and reluctant to forget them. In 1900 he told an editor seeking biographical details that 'until I what you call made a name ... I was kept out of everything decent 'cos "his father keeps a shop" – I believe I'm always introduced so now, that is to say – the remark is invariably made in an undertone.'

No reproofs were to come from Alice. Her education had at least left her in the position of appreciating 'the great and the beautiful' – even if, as a pupil, she might not be able to realize them in her piano playing. 'Dear Alice!' recorded a friend condescendingly, 'how hard she worked at it. She nearly worked her fingers to the bone, and I couldn't think what for.' So Elgar's tutorship was to be in vain – unlike Strauss's when he gave his singing pupil every encouragement to become what the critic Hanslick, enraptured by Pauline's lyric soprano, described as 'his better and more beautiful half'.

Alice's imaginative bent tended more to the literary. She had already had published a two-volume novel, *Marchcroft Manor*, and a long poem; both her prose and her verse were liberally well-meaning but hardly took flight. Did Elgar ever read the novel? – one wonders. And yet he set her passable lyrics time and again – beginning with *The Wind at Dawn*, and then, in the year of their marriage, *O Happy Eyes*. The form was a partsong for unaccompanied chorus, a relatively profitable undertaking in a country that paid its composers little for their creative pains; but the distinguished publishers of choral music, Novellos, were not initially impressed by *O Happy Eyes*. They were right to acknowledge the superior musical poetry of another partsong written at the same time, *My Love Dwelt in a Northern Land*, to words by Andrew Lang, and agreed to print it – not for ready money, but for 100 copies in exchange for the copyright.

Elgar's most successful musical pledge of love to Alice had come a year earlier, before their engagement, in the form of a little piece for violin and piano saluting her knowledge of German in the title, *Liebesgrüss* ('Love's Greeting'). He sold it for two guineas to the publishers Schotts, who insisted on publishing it by the French title of *Salut d'amour*: he was excited to discover, as he wrote to Charles Buck, that 'they do it for *p.f. Solo – vn. & p.f. – orch.* parts & *score*!!! four editions!! gosh!!!' Its exquisite sentiment – rather than sentimentality – made it immediately popular, and by 1897, when Elgar noted that '3,000 copies were sold in the month of January alone', he was wishing he had made some sort of royalty arrangement. The miniature masterpiece was inscribed 'à Carice', a so-called portmanteau word drawn from both Christian names of his bride-to-be.

Salut d'amour suggests tenderness rather than passionate desire, and there is nothing to suggest that physical attraction played a large part in the match. Indeed, save for an unrepeatable piece of gossip reported by a Worcestershire neighbour of Elgar's to a friend of mine, the question of Elgar's sexuality remains under thick Victorian wraps. Basil Maine, writing while Elgar was still alive, defined the marriage as 'a rare and sympathetic friendship in which passion ran deep and calm' – something of a contradiction in terms.

Alice was nearly forty when they met, Elgar seven years her junior, and she then seemed ready to face the spinsterhood that was the lot of so many Victorian daughters left to tend an ailing mother – though not with equanimity. In her long poem, the lot of older, single women was to be visited by 'a sickening sense / Of something they have lost or never known.' The disparity was not to pass unnoticed by the cruelly observant Rosa Burley, who thought that Alice 'seemed almost to belong to a different generation'. For Elgar, Alice undeniably took on certain aspects of a second mother, sharing his own mother's literary tastes and ready to do anything to protect him from the world.

Whether he succeeded because of Alice's uncritical encouragement, or in spite of it, is one of many enigmas surrounding this strange partnership. One thing is certain: his musical confidence increased dramatically from 1889 onwards. He told Charles Buck in February 1889 that he was 'the knight of the rueful countenance no longer' – referring to the melancholy figure of Don Quixote that he must, in his premature world-weariness, have resembled. In May, he summed up: 'This is a time of deep peace & happiness to me after the vain imaginings of so many years & the pessimistic views so often unfolded to you on the Settle highways have vanished! God wot!'

The wedding took place in London at the Brompton Oratory on 8 May 1889. Only William Elgar's brother Henry was present, on Elgar's side, along with his sister Pollie and her husband Will Grafton, in whose house he had lodged before moving on to his oldest sister Lucy (married, by then, to Charles Pipe). Now, having passed on his teaching commitments in Worcestershire, he faced London with Alice. Following a honeymoon on the Isle of Wight, they took a house in Marloes Road, Kensington, until the end of July. They also prepared to occupy the home of one of Alice's Raikes cousins – Oaklands in Upper Norwood – conveniently close to the Crystal Palace. Before then, however, and before Alice's lease on a house in Malvern ran out, there was another summer in Worcestershire to enjoy.

A new company began to take shape. It would find a certain immortality in an orchestral work as yet undreamt of: the *'Enigma' Variations*. The first three 'variations' to enter the frame were all amateur musicians with whom Elgar played that August: two partners in piano trios, the cellist Basil Nevinson and his friend Hew David Steuart-Powell, and Isabel Fitton, the viola-playing daughter of a musical family rare (in Malvern, at least) in having a highly cultured attitude. It was in Malvern that Elgar made several sketches for what was to be his first large-scale composition. Its subject had its origins both in the love, which he shared with his mother, of Longfellow's prose romance *Hyperion* and in Alice's affiliation with Teutonic literature, for the poem that Hyperion reads to his love is *The Black Knight*, a ballad by the popular German poet Johann Ludwig Uhland.

Back in London, it was another chivalrous theme that eventually claimed his attention, and the commission came in January 1890 from William Done – he who had so despised Schumann – down in Worcester. He wanted an orchestral work for the Three Choirs Festival that September. So Done became the first of many figures holding a prominent position in a regional musical organisation to give Elgar the helping hand he later claimed he never had. There was free rein in terms of the subject-matter. The quotation eventually printed at the head of the score came from Keats – 'when CHIVALRY / Lifted up her lance on high' – but it merely encapsulated the essence of what Elgar had in mind: a passage from Sir Walter Scott's *Old Mortality*, where John Graham of Claverhouse expresses his admiration for the French chronicler Froissart and above all Froissart's description of a knight celebrated for 'loyalty to his king, pure faith to his religion, hardihood towards his enemy and fidelity to his lady-love.'

All these elements are there in *Froissart*, even if the general lines of the programme brought forth only the sketchiest of conflicts and development. The succession of splendid themes suggests a variety of different sources. The opening challenge, and its companions, hint at loyal faith, and after their own flexible fashion exude the world of Wagner's *Die Meistersinger*, which Elgar had seen no less than three times in London the previous July. Of the *Ring* cycle, he had so far heard only excerpts from *Die Walküre* in concert, but *Froissart*'s horn-led march in the minor key certainly raises shades of Wagner's vengeful clansman Hunding. A solo clarinet conjures a different world: that of Gilbert and Sullivan's *The Yeomen of the Guard*, with its brilliant overture, which he and Alice went to see on the eve of their wedding.

There is wistfulness in this love-music rather than the kind of sensual passion we hear in Strauss's near-contemporary *Don Juan*. Once again, Elgar stands in relation to Alice as the chivalrous knight, not the ardent lover. Still, the overture as a whole breathes an energy new to Elgar's music. Looking back on it a decade later, when Novellos were finally prepared to publish *Froissart* in full score, he commented: 'What jolly healthy stuff it is – quite shameless in its rude young health! Deary me! was I ever like that?'

He was – but not for long. *Froissart* was completed by the end of July at the Elgars' new London home in West Kensington: sketches, piano score and orchestration had taken a mere two months. Novellos undertook to publish it – though not in full score and with only the string parts engraved, the rest in manuscript – and at the Three Choirs Festival in September, with Elgar playing among the first violins, it was received much as the publisher had rated it – as a work of promise rather than of fulfilment. Financially, prospects were poor, and there was now a baby daughter to support, born less than a month before *Froissart* came into the world and christened Carice after the inscription to her mother on *Salut d'amour*. The London winter was bitter in more ways than one, and, to make things worse, Elgar found himself compelled to commute between London and Worcester, where he had resumed teaching the violin.

Such a retrograde step seems to have epitomized everything that was holding him back. Perhaps that was why he was such a poor teacher. By the following June, he and Alice had left Avonmore Road for Malvern, where Rosa Burley, the new young headmistress of the Mount School, where he taught one day a week, was a sharp observer of his discontent. His reputation preceded their first meeting:

> From various sources I had learned that he was not always good-tempered and that in consequence the girls were afraid of him. Thus it was the custom of every pupil at the end of her lesson to telegraph the state of the emotional atmosphere to her successor and there was one child who enraged him to such an extent that the others had begged that she might be placed last on the list in order to prevent her from making things impossible for them.

She found him shy but proud, uninterested in the pupils' progress, sorry for himself to a degree that verged on the morbid and 'one of the most repressed people it is possible to imagine'. When she came to understand a little more of his ambition as a composer, she realized why he held the mere executors of a truly creative artist's will in such low esteem and, as a member of the ladies' orchestral class he held on a Friday or a Saturday, she had the first inklings of his genius. The work he was rehearsing was a *Serenade for strings*, probably based on the *Three Pieces* of 1888. It was the central *Larghetto* that so impressed Rosa Burley, and it is as personal and private a slow movement as any he wrote, but the writing for strings throughout shows a master's touch. Elgar's special care to divide the melodic interest between the two groups of violins might have been a sympathetic gesture to his father, who had remained among the second violins of the Festival Orchestra while his son had progressed to the firsts.

Teaching may have taken up most of Elgar's time, back in Worcester, but there were new social pleasures, too. Alice's good friend Minnie Baker enlarged the Elgars' circle of acquaintances by introducing them to her brother William Meath Baker, very much of the blustering squirearchical type, and their brother-in-law Richard Baxter Townshend, a classicist and romantic man-of-action frowned upon by 'W.M.B.' as a 'wild Irishman'. Both would furnish 'variation' material on the comic side of the ledger. Another colleague to provide the kindness and support Elgar subsequently denied was Hugh Blair, William Done's assistant at Worcester Cathedral. In December 1891, Elgar played him the *Black Knight* sketches and Blair made him an offer on the spot: 'If you will finish it I will produce it at Worcester.'

Setting to work, Elgar noticed to his amazement that the theme he thought he had dreamed up in summer 1889 for the opening of the work actually belonged to an old sketchbook of a decade earlier. Its ceremonial note, promising so much for a festive premiere, was not to be maintained. Uhland's ballad brings songs and dances of death into a chivalrous setting as a shadow falls over every celebration. The Black Knight defeats his host's son in 'play of spears', dances with his daughter 'in measure weird and dark' and finally destroys the two children at a banquet. That grim conclusion must have had special resonances for Elgar, just as the death of the brother in Mahler's early (1878–80) cantata *Das klagende Lied* had struck home to the young Austrian composer; like Elgar, he had lost two of his own brothers in childhood.

For the dying falls of his second and third movements, Elgar brought into subtle play all the mastery of orchestration he had learnt from the Powick and Glee Club arrangements, and from careful study of other men's music. It was only in the withdrawn pathos of the finale that he allowed the chorus full, unaccompanied expression. Elsewhere their role simply seems superimposed over the self-sufficient orchestral textures: the exquisite march led by clarinet and bassoon that begins the second movement, for instance, sounds wrong when the chorus enters with the words 'To the barrier of the fight', to the same tune.

In 1898, preparing for a second edition of the score, he wrote that he 'intended the work to be a sort of symphony in four divisions founded on the poem – different to anything, in structure, ever done before . . . it's not a proper cantata as the orch. is too important.' In January 1893, Elgar completed the orchestration with his customary ease in less than a month, having worked on the vocal score for much of the previous year; despite the process – to be followed in the cantatas to come – it is clear that he thought in orchestral terms from the start. It is tempting to speculate whether *The Black Knight* would have held a place in the repertoire as a pure orchestral symphony, with the choral part removed; but in 1893, a chorus as well as an orchestra had to be satisfied if the work were to be performed at all. That April, the fulfilment of Blair's promise, with Elgar conducting the Worcester Festival Choral Society, furnished, according to Alice, 'the proudest happiest evening in all ser [i.e. her and Edward's] lives', and the local press acknowledged the scale of his achievement.

The spirit of Wagner is less detectable in *The Black Knight* than one might expect; for in between work on the vocal score in 1892 Elgar and Alice accompanied 'the Mascotte', as they now called Minnie Baker, to Wagner's festival shrine of Bayreuth. There they saw *Die Meistersinger*, *Tristan und Isolde* and two performances of *Parsifal*, then to be seen exclusively at Bayreuth (one interesting offshoot was Elgar's 1894 arrangement of the Good Friday Music from *Parsifal* for a Worcester Girls' High School ensemble of three violins, cello, two pianos and organ). The following August they were in search of Wagner again, this time in Munich; this time, in addition to *Meistersinger* and *Tristan* as well as the early rarity *Die Feen*, and *Tannhäuser*, there was a complete *Ring* cycle.

Elgar may have been sufficiently inspired to brand the 'magic fire' theme from *Die Walküre*, the second opera in the cycle, around the fireplace at Forli, his Malvern home, but the inspiration to compose a new work, when it came, was to issue not from Wagner but from the *Schuhplatt'l* folk dances that he and Alice saw in and around Garmisch, the resort in the Bavarian Alps near Munich where Richard Strauss would later make his home.

On both occasions, the child Carice was left in England with her nurse, to mark her second and third birthdays without her parents. Rosa Burley, whose anecdotes of Munich 1893 make entertaining reading, saw her as a sad little girl:

> *She never smiled or laughed; and when I learned that from the first she had been taught never to make the least noise for fear of disturbing her father, I understood her unnatural look of resignation.*

This only child was hardly to be seen, let alone heard. Not that Elgar did not know how to behave with children of a certain age: a delightful letter from Germany to his sister Pollie's children and the rapport he began to develop around this time with Dora Penny, step-daughter of the newly-married Minnie Baker, prove otherwise. It was simply that, in the Elgars' eyes, their daughter had some growing up to do before she could be a fit companion for her father instead of a prattling nuisance. As soon as she was old enough, Carice was sent as a boarder to a school within easy walking distance of the Elgars' Malvern residence of Forli and stayed there until her early teens. It was all part of Alice's plans for swaddling and protecting 'the Genius' (as Rosa Burley called him) from any distractions.

The Black Knight brought little immediate luck in its wake, only a note of characteristic self-pity that might still be justified as Elgar again took up the role of violinist for the Worcester Festival in September 1893: 'I played 1st violin for the sake of the fee as I cd. obtain no recognition as a composer.' He seems to have taken refuge, as he so often would, in illness; but there was at least a minor commission early the following year, again from the supportive Hugh Blair and marking his first association with the royalty whose court composer he would so spectacularly become. The Duke of York, the future King George V, was to visit Worcester Cathedral in April, and to mark the occasion, Elgar rearranged the slow movement of an unfinished violin sonata as *Sursum corda* for strings, organ, timpani and brass. Perhaps because of its origins, Elgar's first piece of ceremonial pomp bears his most personal signature: the main melody has much in common with the slow movement of the *Serenade for strings*.

Apart from that, and an *Organ Sonata* for Blair which is less elaborate, and more introspective, than reports of the dedicatee's fumbling first efforts might lead one to expect – it is true Blair received the finished manuscript rather late in the day – there were only trifles to occupy Elgar's compositional time. One turned out to be a real charmer: a set of six *Scenes from the Bavarian Highlands*, based on the traditional songs and dances witnessed on the three German holidays (the third took place in 1894). Perhaps, once again, Elgar should have left his own tributes as dances and forgotten about the song element, for out of the three numbers he suggested to Novellos as suitable for orchestra alone, the choral parts of the full first version sit clumsily alongside the melody-bearing orchestra in '*Lullaby*' and '*The Marksman*'. The part-writing is more accomplished – touching, even – in two of the original numbers that rely more on choral effect, '*False Love*' and '*On the Alm*', and is proof, along with two partsongs of the same year (*The Snow* and *Fly, Singing Bird*), also to texts by Alice, that Elgar was less clumsy with words when there were no orchestral ideas to take precedence. By the same token, he was no master wordsmith to rank with Purcell; that accolade would eventually go, several decades on, to Benjamin Britten.

The major task of the mid-1890s was a long time in evolving. The influential Midlands conductor Charles Swinnerton Heap was sufficiently impressed by *The Black Knight* to invite Elgar to conduct it in Wolverhampton. He also wanted a new work for chorus and orchestra, and Elgar looked over possible subjects. But that was in December 1894, and it was not until the following autumn that he could offer a premiere at the North Staffordshire Festival in October 1896. By then, Elgar had already accepted a commission for the Worcester Three Choirs Festival, due to take place only a few weeks before the Staffordshire event.

Suddenly he had his hands full. The theme of the Worcester commission had been decided in discussion with the Malvern clergyman Edward Capel Cure – the story of the blind man healed, from the Gospel of St John – and the Norse sagas had already seized hold of his imagination shortly after Swinnerton Heap had first approached him.

Unfortunately he chose not a Wagnerian view of Norse mythology, but Longfellow's; and then, saddling himself with a text that lacked the shining virtue of the original sagas – clarity of narration – he cut those very aspects of it that helped to evoke a barbaric past. Rosa Burley may have seen him mock Alice for her prudery over certain aspects of Wagner's operas in Munich, but he was hardly less squeamish. At any rate, Olaf, standard-bearer of Christianity, was shorn of the violence with which he displayed his religious zeal and of his ardour as a lover.

Even so, *Scenes from the Saga of King Olaf* contained some of Elgar's bravest attempts at a dramatic sweep, on a scale vaster than anything he had written so far. Again, foursquare choral writing blocked the way forward at times, but Elgar's orchestral imagination at its most fastidious graced much of the music for the nature-loving Olaf and his brides-to-be (too much so, perhaps, for the vengeful Gudrun).

It was the same with the Biblical tale for Worcester, *Lux Christi* (eventually renamed *The Light of Life* since the title reeked of Rome as far as the Anglicans were concerned). Here the disparity between choral and orchestral writing was all the more marked following the chain of inspired ideas in the opening Meditation for orchestra alone, although he managed to sustain the introspective mood impressively through the first five numbers.

The London critics were there at that Worcester premiere, and *The Sunday Times* was perceptive enough to praise as exceptional Elgar's 'sense of proportion and tone colour, and his knowledge of effect.' Inevitably, though, the more ambitious *King Olaf* took pride of place as the harbinger of genius. The Staffordshire first night did not go entirely smoothly: the tenor missed the last rehearsal, and seems to have thrown Elgar, conducting the work, to such an extent at one point that the performance was saved only by the orchestral leader. Few in the audience noticed, however, and the unanimous critical praise brought problems of its own, well articulated by Harry Acworth, a Malvern neighbour who had worked without much success on the *Olaf* libretto:

> *In one respect I am sorry for you. You have now the obligation of living up to a great reputation, a reputation which if I read the critics aright places you at the head of living composers, & high wrought expectations are difficult to satisfy – & such all your work will henceforth evoke.*

This is a clear indication that success did not come overnight with the '*Enigma*' *Variations* two years later, but it brought Elgar little initial satisfaction. For the first time, he found himself in that ambivalent position of both courting success and shrinking away from it; and his first reaction – as he buried his head in his mother's lap and told her he could not face the exposure – was to shrink away.

1897 saw a consolidation both of outward triumphs and of a new friendship on which he could depend for refuge. The triumphs were a Crystal Palace performance of *King Olaf* under August Manns in April and the fulfilment of two commissions for Queen Victoria's Diamond Jubilee: an *Imperial March*, with claims to being the real *Pomp and Circumstance* No.1 and a short cantata about St George and the Dragon. Yet its success, in a half-empty Crystal Palace, left Elgar with heavy expenses to offset. *The Banner of St George*, his first major work on a subject not of his choosing, turned out to be little more than a competent *pièce d'occasion* – even if it had the virtue of a sensitive opening. True royalist and conservative though he already was, Elgar would probably not have undertaken the task had it not promised a certain much-needed financial reward. Unfortunately, if predictably, such bread-and-butter fare was to become fuel to the fire of those who choose to stereotype him as a callow imperialist.

He certainly gave of his best for another official duty, a setting of the Anglican *Te Deum and Benedictus* for George Sinclair, the organist of Hereford Cathedral where the Three Choirs Festival would take place that year. Elgar obliged Sinclair with an opening theme more memorable in its clear-cut vigour than anything in *The Banner of St George*, and subjected to dreamy, nostalgic variation in the unexpected and deeply moving quiet coda of the *Te Deum*; the theme played a linking role, too, in the *Benedictus*.

It was as an admirer of the *Te Deum* that the central figure of the '*Enigma*' *Variations*, August Johannes Jaeger, made his characteristically enthusiastic entry into Elgar's life. Jaeger was a German musician who had come to England with his family in 1878. Elgar's complaints about the lack of encouragement in his own life now seem insignificant, when compared to the circumstance of Jaeger's career. For although he was a fine pianist and violinist, his father had made him swear that he would never perform in public. Thus he joined the staff at Novellos as a lesser manager and adviser in matters artistic.

Jaeger's estimate of himself in a letter to Elgar written in

1900 was as 'a poor chap who works hard in the interest of English music and is fool enough to be enthusiast (for which he is only laughed at)'. But he had to 'wax enthusiastic over *something* – it's part of my life' and in Elgar's music he found his cause. Elgar, in turn, was glad to find someone who understood his music. He had already confided in young Nicholas Kilburn, who had championed his *King Olaf* with modest resources up in Durham: 'alas! for us musicians there are so few pioneers like yourself who will stand up & say "this thing is worthy" – until they have been told a thousand times.' He was now able to enlarge the point with Jaeger:

> . . . *please do not think I am a disappointed person, either commercially or artistically – what I feel is the utter want of* sympathy – *they, principally the critics, lump me with people I abhor* – mechanics. *Now my music, such as it is, is alive, you say it has heart – I always say to my wife (over any piece or passage of my work that pleases me): 'if you cut that it would bleed!' You seem to see that – but who else does?*

After four months' intensive correspondence with Elgar – airing gossip, discussing the new music and declaiming the motto '*Heart* above all things!' – Jaeger's greeting on the eve of 1898 was auspicious. He dismissed what was to be an increasingly unnecessary negative vein on Elgar's part, and added:

> *Your time of universal recognition will come. You have virtually achieved more toward that end in* one year *than others of the foremost English composers in a decade! So once more '*Glück auf!*' and let us have your masterpiece by & by.*

CHAPTER 3
TRIUMPH
(1898–1900)

+ A tale of the Malvern hills
+ Depression
+ 'Friends pictured within'
+ Richter to the rescue
+ Gerontius

The masterpiece for which Jaeger was hoping might have emerged more swiftly than it did, had Elgar only been able to do what he wanted with the next festival commission. The offer this time came from Leeds, and Elgar wanted to dispense with a chorus in favour of writing 'perhaps a series of illustrative movements for orchestra with "Mottoes" from English history'. It is tempting to speculate that the form might have been a theme and a series of variations, with national heroes 'pictured within'. The chorus, however, could not be dismissed for so grand an occasion: as Elgar told Alfred Littleton, the chairman at Novellos, 'I have hinted at other things but it seems they wish a cantata.'

At least there was something of a 'living wage' in it: £100 for all rights, agreed by mid-January 1898. The subject, too, had the private roots necessary for Elgar's music to flourish. The previous August, he and Alice had stayed with his seventy-six-year-old mother in a small village near the Malvern Hills, and the view of the Herefordshire Beacon, with its earthworks built, according to legend, by the great British warrior Caractacus as a defence against Claudius's Roman army, gave the old lady an idea. 'I said Oh! Ed. Look at the lovely old Hill. Can't we write some *tale* about it. I quite long to have something worked up about it; so full of ... historical interest ... [He replied] you *can* "do it yousef

Mother". He held my hand with a firm grip: "do," he said.' Ann Elgar declared her day was past for such things; but that local aspect of the Caractacus legend soon became a vital inspiration as Elgar began work on the cantata. According to Rosa Burley, he 'tramped over the hills and went along the Druid path from end to end, along the top of the hills.' At the northern end, he found the retreat that was to become the most personally significant of all his homes, temporary or otherwise: a cottage on the country estate of Birchwood, negotiated for short-term lease.

The wood that Elgar knew there – and which came to be associated with *Caractacus* through another theme long since invented but now delicately fashioned as the 'Woodland Interlude' before Scene Three – has gone, although a subsequent plantation now fully-grown makes a fine substitute for the visitor's imagination. Most important, though, is the view, which remains the same: a magnificent sweep along the backbone of the Malvern Hills, with the British camp clearly visible to the south. Here was inspiration made constantly visible.

The personal aspect of *Caractacus* goes hand in hand with a characteristically Elgarian subject of defeat and resignation. Led captive to Rome, Caractacus remembers his liberty in poignant terms: 'I made old Caractacus stop as if broken down,' wrote Elgar to Jaeger, '& choke & say 'woodlands' again because I'm so madly devoted to my woods.' The quartet that follows, in which the clement Emperor Claudius joins the calm but peaceful sentiments of the captives, owes something to Elgar's admiration of the Act Three quintet from Wagner's *Die Meistersinger*. It stands alongside the finest music in the cantata, which includes the many moments of nature-poetry and a surprisingly fine duet to serve the invented love-interest of the piece, Caractacus's daughter and her druidical suitor.

The general sweep could hardly fail to impress, too: when Elgar wrote to Kilburn in March 1898 'it "flows on somehow" like the other best of me,' he might have been thinking of the first half of *The Light of Life* and the music of *King Olaf* from the 'Wraith of Odin' sequence onwards, a strain which parts of *Caractacus* resume so impressively.

Also on the credit side is a Triumphal March for the Romans, which was a little on the brazen side for the hypersensitive Jaeger. He found it hard to bear 'those Heathens à la Moussorgsky' brought to the fore in the wave of Russomania then sweeping London under the banner of the enterprising young conductor Henry Wood. By a strange irony, *Caractacus* was shortly to be much in demand to mark the progress of the less-than-glorious British enterprise in the Boer War, with *The Banner of St George* trotted out to celebrate the Relief of Mafeking in 1900.

None of this was Elgar's fault. What he did allow was a preposterous coda to *Caractacus*, making good the general's failure with an apotheosis of great Britain's achievements over the centuries since the fall of Rome. Harry Acworth, whose work on *King Olaf* and the rest of *Caractacus* had proved of average quality, had now sunk to the level of patriotic doggerel. Jaeger, dealing with proofs of the final scene in June 1898, objected to the words 'menial' and 'jealous' being applied to foreigners. Elgar asked Acworth to tone it down, explaining to Jaeger 'I *did* suggest we dabble in patriotism in the Finale, when lo! the *worder* (that's good!) instead of merely paddling his feet goes & gets naked & wallows in it.' Two weeks later, he was less conciliatory: 'England for the English is all I say – hands off! there's nothing apologetic about me.'

In any case, the national spirit needed appeasement. The following year was to witness Victoria's eightieth birthday – to be marked on Elgar's part only by what he called 'a *Madrigalian* partsong' 'to order' – and he cannily sought permission (granted) to dedicate *Caractacus* to the Queen and Empress. The Leeds premiere on 5 October was a grand occasion, not one likely to put Elgar at his ease when, as conductor, he came to deal with the details of performance. Rosa Burley duly noted the strain, observing that the audience were 'a good deal less clerical, less County' than at the Three Choirs Festival and 'a good deal more fashionable and opulent.'

If *Caractacus* 'frightened' Elgar while he was engaged in the composition, as he perhaps rather artfully avowed to Kilburn and Jaeger on two separate occasions, it hardly overwhelmed the assembled company and was accepted instead, rather placidly, as a 'triumph'. 'Mr. Elgar has not inaptly been dubbed "the Rudyard Kipling of the Musicians" ' trumpeted *The Court Journal* , a publication as unlikely to notice the darker shades in Kipling's poetry as it was to stress the introspective side of Elgar's music.

In spite of favourable reviews, his mood turned black, as it so often did after the strain of creativity and performance. Back in Malvern, he was annoyed with the suggestion from Novellos of another *Banner of St George* for a vital new commission, this time from Birmingham for the festival in 1900, and wrote to Jaeger in late October, tarring him with the brush of his company:

> *I'm not happy at all in fact never was more miserable in all my life: I don't see that I've done any good at all: if I write a tune you all say it's commonplace – if I don't, you all say it's rot. – well I've written* Caractacus, *earning thro' it* 15/-d. *a week while doing it & that's all – now if I will write any easy, small choral-society work for Birmingham, using the fest. as an advt. – your firm will be 'disposed to consider it' – but my own natural bent I must choke off ... I tell you I am sick of it all: why can't I be encouraged to do decent stuff & not hounded into triviality?*

The discouraged tone was a familiar one, and to be maintained, whether he was creating or not, throughout the years to come.

There were to be moments of genuine despair; but more often than not, the frequent complaint that he was 'sick of music' was a childish cry for help. One of Jaeger's no-nonsense retorts was exactly what he needed: 'Papperlapapp! That's what Wagner said when he was creating his crushing efforts of genius.'

Sure enough, the day after that letter in which Elgar had told Jaeger he was 'never more miserable in my life' and the very evening of the day he sent another letter announcing his intentions to retire from the public eye, he sat down at the piano and extemporized. Alice liked the new tune he had just picked out, and in his own words 'asked with a sound of approval, "What is that?" I answered, "Nothing – but something might be made of it." '

He remembered Hew David Steuart-Powell's piano runs before joining in the trios Elgar had played with Nevinson and Steuart-Powell in the first summer of his marriage; making a variation on the theme like one of those practise toccatas, but 'chromatic beyond H.D.S.-P.'s liking,' he remarked 'Powell would have done this.' That led to Nevinson the cellist's part in the proceedings – a singing variation made for the cellos. A boisterous treatment of the theme with an emphatic final slam led Alice to observe 'it is exactly the way W.M.B. [William Meath Baker, Minnie's brother] goes out of the room.' And she added, 'You are doing something which I think has never been done before.'

She was right. Variation form in itself was nothing new, though it had no doubt taken more recent examples breathing human warmth into a potentially academic structure to turn Elgar's thoughts in that direction. Chief among them were Dvořák's *Symphonic Variations* and the charming finale of Tchaikovsky's *Third Suite*, which must have been very much on Elgar's mind that October as it had followed the *Caractacus* premiere in an extraordinarily long Leeds Festival programme. First after Alice to hear news of fresh inspiration was Jaeger:

> *I have sketched a set of variations (orkestry) on an original theme: the Variations themselves have amused me because I've labelled 'em with the nicknames of my particular friends* – you are Nimrod [the Biblical 'mighty hunter'; Jaeger is the German word for 'hunter']. *That is to say I've written the variations each one to represent the mood of the 'party' – I've liked to imagine the 'party' writing the var: him (or her) self & have written what I think they would have written – if they were asses enough to compose – it's a quaint idee & the result is amusing to those behind the scenes & won't affect the hearer who 'nose nuffin'. what think you?*

Looking back on the genesis of the *Variations* in 1908, Elgar described them as 'commenced in a spirit of humour & continued in deep seriousness'. Nothing could be more serious than the characterization of Jaeger, eventually to be the very heart of the work. 'I have omitted your outside manner & have seen only the good, lovable honest SOUL in the middle of you!' he later revealed, though both men knew the specific roots of the 'Nimrod' Variation.

Elgar revealed half the truth in his notes for pianola rolls of the *Variations* made in 1928 (the source of the other quotations reproduced below), when he described the 'Nimrod' variation as 'the record of a long summer evening talk, when my friend discoursed eloquently on the slow movements of Beethoven, and said that no one could approach Beethoven at his best in this field, a view with which I cordially concurred. It will be noticed that the opening bars are made to suggest the slow movement of the *Eighth Sonata* (*Pathétique*).'

What Jaeger had actually said about Beethoven during that long summer evening concerned his years of struggle: it was meant as an encouragement to Elgar not to give up composing, as he threatened, and it obviously did some good. Alice, by contrast, served only provide 'romantic and delicate' embroideries to both halves of the theme – its limping minor-key opening and the 'woodland' colour of its clarinet-led second half – as Variation One.

Other feminine influence had entered the picture more recently. In late 1897, he and Alice had thought of returning to London. One incentive to stay was the founding of a new society for Elgar to conduct, the Worcestershire Philharmonic – 'a sort of toy I suppose for a petulant child,' he wrote with unusual self-knowledge. Two genteel ladies, Martina Hyde and Winifred Norbury, were the society secretaries, and although the exquisitely scored Variation Eight purports to be a portrait of Winifred Norbury and the country house in which she lived, it originally bore the title '(2 secys)'. Lady Mary Lygon served on the aristocratic committee. Neither her work, along with 'W.N.', on the score of *Caractacus* – one of the rare occasions when Alice allowed outside help – nor her attractive personality, would be enough to account for Elgar's heartbreaking clarinet quotation of a theme from Mendelssohn's *Calm Sea and Prosperous Voyage* in the variation originally marked with three asterisks.

Lady Mary was indeed about to embark on a sea voyage to join her brother in Australia, but Rosa Burley, not much given to romanticizing, insists that 'Edward told me quite clearly and unequivocally whom it represented and I always supposed that his reason for witholding this lady's name was that extremely intimate and personal feelings were concerned. . . . The present dedication to Lady Mary Lygon (later Trefusis) was really the result of a false inference which Edward rather surprisingly allowed.' So Helen Weaver ('Lovely Maiden Lost'?) is the most plausible candidate for the *Variations*' most introspective sequences.

Lighter-hearted vignettes bear witness to other relative newcomers. The serious conversation of Richard (son of Matthew) Arnold is 'continually broken up by whimsical and witty remarks' from the woodwind instruments. 'Uncouth' timpani and lower strings represent unmusical architect Arthur Troyte Griffith's maladroit attempts to play the piano (although Jerrold Northrop Moore thinks that Variation Seven is the depiction of a thunderstorm encountered by Elgar and Troyte during a walk in the Malvern Hills). Elgar had long known George Sinclair, organist of Hereford Cathedral, but the recently-observed antics of his bulldog Dan were the real subject of the Sinclair variation: his 'falling down the steep bank into the river Wye (bar 1); his paddling up stream to find a landing place (bars 2 and 3) and his rejoicing bark on landing (second half of bar 5).'

Femininity further redressed the balance in the tall and elegant portrait of viola-player Isabel Fitton and a featherlight Intermezzo lending Dora Penny a nickname out of Mozart's *Cosi fan tutte* and wryly imitating her stammer ('I *have* orchestrated you well,' wrote Elgar in one of his many playful letters to the girl). These two characterizations had much in common with the elegance of the *Chanson de matin* Elgar composed around the same time, itself a companion-piece to the darker, more virile *Chanson de nuit* of two years earlier. He suppressed his own feminine side, however, in the rumbustious self-assertion of the *Variations'* self-portrait finale.

That confident note was little in evidence as he worked on the *Variations*. Early in 1899, he wrote to Nicholas Kilburn (a potential 'variation' who had to be sacrificed, along with Ivor Atkins, the new organist of Worcester Cathedral – another lifelong friend): 'We have been thro' a time of much searching of heart with the result that I am going to write a little more music before going back to my teaching . . . I have completed nearly a set of Variations for orchestra which I like – but commercially nothing.'

The prospects, in one respect, were brighter than he thought. In February, he sent the manuscript of the orchestral score to Richter through Richter's orchestral manager N. Vert, whose prompt reply was that Richter would study the score on his return from tour, declaring, 'he shall be only too pleased to promote the work of an English artiste.' It was through Richter that Elgar had first come to know his Brahms and Wagner, but he also realized the great man's reputation as a champion of English music (the notorious critic Eduard Hanslick complained that Richter had turned Vienna's musical scene into a 'little English colony'). The result was positive: Richter set down the *Variations* for a concert in London's St James's Hall on 19 June. After he had returned the manuscript, the magic word 'Enigma' appeared on the opening page in Jaeger's handwriting.

Pressed for an explanation by the writer of the programme note for the forthcoming concert, Charles Ainslie Barry, Elgar gave the elusive response that has provided food for journalistic speculation ever since:

> The Enigma I will not explain – its 'dark saying' must be left unguessed, and I warn you that the apparent connexion between the Variations and the Theme is often of the slightest texture; further, through and over the whole set another and larger theme 'goes' but is not played.

Among innumerable candidates proposed for the 'larger theme' was 'Auld Lang Syne', a sentiment neatly in tune with the nostalgic overtones of the work. The conductor Christopher Seaman ingeniously engages an alphabetical code-system of the kind popular at the turn of the century to discover the dedication 'à Carice' in the theme's first notes, a fine notion – although it could pertain either to the wife, as she was hailed in 'Salut d'amour', or the daughter. Darker speculations on the extra-musical possibilities of a 'larger theme' are prompted by Elgar himself, who referred Barry to two Maeterlinck plays in which the unseen principal character was Death. When he quoted the theme in *The Music Makers* thirteen years later, he wrote that in 1899 it had stood for his 'sense of the loneliness of the artist'. And that is probably as much of an answer as we deserve.

The layer of mystification irritated many of the critics at the London premiere, although most praised the substance, the structure and the orchestration of the *Variations*. More telling than short-term praise was the number of performances the work received shortly afterwards. The first, long planned, was at Little Brighton near Liverpool in July, where the promising composer and conductor Granville Bantock asked Elgar to take charge of his orchestra – 'so jolly to conduct – enthusiastic and hard-workers.'

In the interim, Jaeger had persuaded Elgar to extend the finale by 100 bars to the form in which we know it today, buttressed by an additional organ part: too late, as it turned out, for Little Brighton, but in time for the Worcester Festival in September, with Elgar again conducting. 'The performance of the

Variations was really good especially *you*,' he wrote to Jaeger, 'slow and fine it sounded. Finale sounded gorgeous.' The occasion provided some of the 'friends pictured within' to exercise their provincial largesse. One came up to Rosa Burley and said, 'I'm a variation. Are you?' – to which came the wry retort, 'no, I'm not a variation. I'm the theme.'

The work soon took on a new lease of life. Richter showed how highly he thought of it by giving another London performance, and included it in his first season as principal conductor of Manchester's Hallé Orchestra. Henry Wood, who had hoped to give the first performance, finally featured it at the Queen's Hall in 1901; London heard it again the following year when the Court Orchestra of Meiningen, once under the direction of the great Hans von Bülow and his distinguished assistant the young Richard Strauss, visited England with Fritz Steinbach. In Russia, a distinguished pupil of Tchaikovsky, Alexander Siloti, conducted the *Variations* in St Petersburg and Moscow in 1904 – by which time the work had become very much international property.

Depression did not, for once, follow in the wake of that 1899 premiere. Elgar faced the prospect of another distinguished first performance at the Norwich Festival, conducting the newly-popular contralto Clara Butt in a song-cycle for soloist and orchestra, *Sea Pictures*. There had been little evidence of Elgar's affinity either with words or the sea up to this point, and yet away from the forced rhetoric of '*Sabbath Morning at Sea*' and '*The Swimmer*' – a gift, presumably, for Clara Butt's more histrionic talents – Elgar's more introspective musical personality works small wonders on indifferent poetry. '*In Haven*' is a tiny gem, a delicate refashioning of a song he had set to Alice's words as '*Lute Song*' in 1897, and was duly encored at the premiere to the poet's joy; yet it is '*Where corals lie*', with its remote, hypnotic conjuring of another world, that has become the best-loved of all Elgar's songs.

An initial meeting with the prima donna in January had been abruptly terminated when Miss Butt, enjoying her bath, ordered her companion Madame Snella to send the visitor away; but that was a misunderstanding and by October, it was 'call me Clara'. Dressed to resemble a mermaid, she gave the Norwich audience what it wanted. 'The cycle went marvellously well,' Elgar wrote to Jaeger, '& we were recalled four times – I think – after that I got disgusted & lost count – She sang *really well*.'

There were other rewards in a Sheffield performance of *King Olaf*, where Elgar heard a 'superlative' chorus realize the effects he intended for the first time – '& very terrifying they are.' The realization may have played a part in the demands he was to make of the chorus in his next major work, initiated in November by a commission from Birmingham for the prestigious festival of 1900. The new 'oratorio' would embrace two themes he had already sketched, one for a symphony celebrating General Gordon, which was eventually abandoned, the other (curiouser and curiouser) entered into Sinclair's visitors' book as a tune for bulldog Dan in pensive mood. The first idea directly related to the new project, however, was written down for Jaeger's benefit in November and headed with a Biblical quotation: 'Then Jesus said unto him – "That thou doest do quickly" – he (Judas) went immediately out; *and it was night*!' Judas's betrayal, the failure of a thinking man, had clearly taken imaginative hold; but as the year drew to a close, the idea of placing Judas's predicament within a framework of *Ring*-like dimensions fostered only despair at the impossibility of the scheme being ready for Birmingham.

Rescue came on New Year's Day 1900, in the practical shape of a visit from the chairman of the Birmingham Festival Orchestral Sub-Committee, George Hope Johnstone. Elgar reverted to an idea he had already discussed with Father Bellasis of the Birmingham Oratory to adapt the guiding light of his early years, Cardinal Newman's poem *The Dream of Gerontius*. Abridged to a manageable length, in further consultation with Newman's executor, the simple fable of an everyman-figure's death and his Soul's journey to the afterlife provided a feasible framework for a two-part festival offering. In early February, with 'the Birmingham work' already accepted for publication by Novellos, Elgar told Jaeger: 'I am setting Newman's *Dream of Gerontius* – awfully solemn and mystic . . . I say that Judas theme will *have* to be used up for death & despair in this work – so don't peach.' The theme – which furnished chromatic torments much in the manner of Wagner's *Parsifal* – was used to introduce the Angel of the Agony in Part Two.

The Prelude, avoiding a glimpse of the afterlife, and confining itself to the thoughts and musical ideas passing through the protagonist's mind as in Strauss's tone-poem *Tod und Verklärung* (Death and Transfiguration) (1890), provided a distinguished home for the two ideas already sketched: thoughtful Dan became the theme on woodwind against rocking harp labelled 'Prayer' in Jaeger's subsequent analysis, and the noble idea for the symphony furnished a climactic consolation to return for the later stages of the earthly chorus's farewell at the end of the first part. As the Prelude indicated, however, there was much pain and suffering to endure first, and much of it would seem to be Elgar's own – his mental torture as well as the physical ailments that afflicted him at times of uncertainty (about the cowled figure on solo viola, horns and bassoons, he told Jaeger that it could be called 'Sleep' – 'but it's the ghastly troubled sleep of a sick man').

Gerontius, in other words, was in part a self-portrait, and the demands Elgar placed on his tenor soloist were the most strenuous and heartfelt of any of his solo parts. Elgar envisaged Gerontius as 'a man like us, not a Priest or a Saint, but a *sinner*, a repentant one of course but still no end of a *worldly* man in his life, & now brought to book. Therefore I've not filled his part with Church tunes and rubbish but a good, healthy full-blooded romantic, remembered worldliness, so to speak.'

He finished the piano score of Part One in March 1900, and then gave Jaeger a special preview of the Angel's Farewell, which was to crown the entire work 'for your own Angel to sing as a peace offering to HER – not you – you old – Nimrod.' Jaeger's wife, a fine amateur musician, duly sang it at home, and even without the benefit of the ineffable orchestration that helps the soloist to tread air, Jaeger immediately put his finger on the special quality of this 'finale':

> *It has a character unlike anything else in music as far as I know. Simple as it is, its very simplicity is its wonder – so aloof from things mundane, so haunting and strangely fascinating . . . I can imagine how you wish this extraordinary song sung: without any kind of passion & singer's 'points', without any hurrying or working up to climaxes . . .*

Immortalized by such great singers as Janet Baker and Kathleen Ferrier, the Farewell still remains justly famous in its own right, but shines in its true context, a perfect elaboration and enrichment of the 'strange refreshment' that begins Part Two. Birchwood again worked its magic on the other-worldly quality of that tender string introduction, for Elgar returned there to work on the orchestration in the summer. From there he wrote to Kilburn, 'on our hillside night after night looking across our "illimitable" horizon (pleonasm!) I've seen in thought the Soul go up and have written my own heart's blood into the score.'

Jaeger continued to play his part not just as Elgar's enthusiastic spur but as a clear-sighted critic. When he studied the music completed either side of the great '*Praise to the Holiest*' chorus of Part Two at the end of May, he declared:

> *Oh! I am half undone, & I tremble after the* tremendous *exaltation I have gone through. I don't pretend to know* every-thing *that has been written since Wagner breathed his last in Venice seventeen years ago, but I have not seen or heard* anything *since* Parsifal *that has stirred me, and spoken to me with the trumpet tongue of genius as has this part of your latest, & by far greatest work.*

The great chorus itself, bearing no relation to the 'Ancient and Modern' tune, overwhelmed him, too, although he found it took some time to grasp its 'vast, pyramidical' structure. One thing, however, was to worry him. He felt that Elgar had shirked the moment where the soul of Gerontius for a split-second sees its God, just as he had avoided the crucial conflicts of *King Olaf* and *Caractacus*, or for that matter the point in *The Light of Life* at which the blind man regains his sight. This was a more serious matter. Wagner, wrote Jaeger, would have made it 'the *climax* of *expression* in the work, especially in the ORCHESTRA, which HERE should surely shine as a medium for *portraying emotions*!' After much cajoling, Elgar eventually gave way, and inserted the grand climax of the work leading 'for *one semi-quaver* value *ffffff*zzzz . . . the one glimpse into the Unexpressible.'

Elgar put the finishing touches to the full score on 3 August 1900. He sealed the manuscript with a quotation from Ruskin's *Sesame and Lilies*:

> *This is the best of me; for the rest, I ate, and drank, and slept, loved and hated, like another; my life was as the vapour and is not; but this I saw and knew; this, if anything of mine, is worth your memory.*

The Birmingham first performance that September could not have dealt a more devastating blow. Richter was again the conductor, but his copy of the score, owing to printing vagaries, reached him far too late. Both his preparation and the rehearsal time were inadequate; two out of the three soloists proved quite unequal to the spiritual demands of their parts; and, worst of all, the Birmingham Festival Chorus's conductor, the faithful Charles Swinnerton Heap, had died, leaving their instruction to the hands of the now aged and infirm William Stockley. Several times they went seriously out of tune in unaccompanied passages, and the fiendish Demons' Chorus brought virtual collapse. The critics, to do them credit, saw through the melee; but that was little consolation to Elgar. He wrote to Jaeger:

> *I have worked hard for forty years & at the last, Providence denies me a decent hearing of my work: so I submit – I always said God was against art & I still believe it. . . . I have allowed my heart to open once – it is now shut against every religious feeling & every soft, gentle impulse* for ever.

This time the sincerity of his words, and the hints of suicide that followed, contained no idle threat. Jaeger had already seen to it, however, that Julius Buths, conductor of the Lower Rhenish Music Festivals, received a score of the '*Enigma*' *Variations* and from Buths was to come the helping hand that *Gerontius* needed. When the wise and kindly Johnstone wrote to Novellos that 'it *is* one of the greatest works ever written by an Englishman & I hope some day it may have full justice done to it,' he little thought that justice would come from the enterprising, forward-looking world of musical Germany.

CHAPTER 4

THE POWER
AND THE GLORY
(1901–8)

- ◆ *Pomp and ceremony*
- ◆ *Honours at home and abroad*
- ◆ *Biblical sagas*
- ◆ *Italy*
- ◆ *A symphony at last*

Any man who could declare in a single letter: 'I wish I were dead over and over again – but I dare not, for the sake of my relatives, do the job myself' one moment and: 'we are very well & jolly' the next, might justifiably be accused of self-indulgence. More of the same met only with the response it deserved from Jaeger. If, as Elgar complained, his heart beat time 'to most marvellous music – unwritten alas! & ever to be so,' then as far as Jaeger was concerned, he deserved 'no pity or thanks, but everlasting chastisement and contempt, you villain. I often wish you were not so comfortably off, able to play golf, kiting, riding &c &c.' Financially, it is true, prospects were not good for the Elgars, and as Littleton, the Novellos chairman, had admitted, *Gerontius* was, as yet, a commercial failure. Yet at the time of writing to Jaeger, Elgar had accepted an honorary doctorate from Cambridge University, initiated by the composer he most despised, Stanford, and for which friends clubbed together together to buy the robes. He was also considering an overture for London's Royal Philharmonic Society, and its mood could not have been further removed either from the spirituality of *Gerontius* or his own avowed depression. 'I call it "Cockayne" & it's cheerful and Londony – "stout and steaky",' he wrote to Jaeger on 4 November. Cockaigne, he told Richter helpfully, 'is the old, humorous (classical) name for London and from it we get the term Cockney.'

One idea, *scherzando* in cockney-sparrow style, was jotted down for Jaeger's benefit the following February. In the context of the overture, it turned out to be a cheeky derivation of the work's big tune, one of the first to bear a marking that became a firm favourite, '*nobilmente*', and the derivation stood in relation to the big tune much as the apprentices' mockery had to their masters' voices in Wagner's Overture to *Die Meistersinger* (although Elgar claimed that the real source was Delibes' ballet *Sylvia*). More lyrical writing in an introspective vein for strings would allow Elgar to withdraw, as he always did, from the hurly-burly; but he carried off the stoutest and steakiest music of all, a brass-band procession, in brilliant style, following it up with a bedraggled Salvation Army troop and engaging his usually wistful pair of clarinets for the comic purpose.

The mingling and meeting of themes was carried out with far more assurance than in *Froissart*, providing another step on the road to the symphony he had so long wanted – but feared – to write. Another *nobilmente* idea fit for that prospective symphony had already appeared at the beginning of 1902. 'Gosh! man I've got a tune in my head,' he confided parenthetically to Jaeger; though if we are to believe a remark he later made to Edward VII, that tune had been in his head since childhood. It was the trio of a march, one of two jotted down not for any specific ceremonial purposes but simply because, as he later explained, 'I did not see why the ordinary quick march should not be treated on a large scale in the way that the waltz, the old-fashioned slow march and even the polka have been treated by the great composers.'

He was heading towards a kind of public office involuntarily. All these new ideas were connected with the city that he had so recently professed to hate, not the countryside he loved. The contrariness was typical, but London was gaining the upper hand, as can be gleaned from his correspondence. 'I'm not coming to London . . . because I hate it' (December 1898). 'I really prefer London' (May 1899). 'I am bored to death with commonplace ass-music down here – the bucolics are all right when they don't attempt more than eat, drink & Sleep but beyond those things they fail' (from Worcester, November 1900). 'Oh so lovely but solus 'cos I can't find anybody here foolheaded enough to eat bread & cheese & drink beer – they've all got livers & apparently live in the country 'cos they can't afford to be swells in a town' (from Malvern, 1902). He remained loyal to local friends, exemplified by his rapid orchestration of *Emmaus*, a cantata by the Gloucester Cathedral organist Herbert Brewer, in the wake of Brewer's near-breakdown in the summer of 1901, and the newly-discovered art of bicycle riding with Rosa Burley gave him the pleasure of discovering every Worcestershire byway. But there were new, cosmopolitan influences on the scene, chief among them Frank Schuster. Jewish, homosexual and what the Americans would call 'a honey', Schuster entertained an enormous social circle, partly at his London home, more often at a tastefully-furnished retreat, known as 'The Hut', by the Thames near Maidenhead, and in the words of Siegfried Sassoon was 'something more than a *patron* of music because he loved music as much as it is humanly possible to do.'

The other close friend was Alfred Rodewald, also wealthy by virtue of being a textile magnate but more directly involved with music than Schuster; he was the gifted conductor of the Liverpool Orchestral Society, and it was to 'dear Rodey' that Elgar dedicated the first of his two marches. Now called *Pomp and Circumstance* – after lines in Shakespeare's *Othello* which, like Kipling's famous and much-misunderstood poem *Recessional*, envisage a farewell to arms rather than a continuation of military glory – they were first performed in Liverpool by Rodewald and his orchestra on 19 October 1901.

It was not until four days later in London, however, that *Pomp and Circumstance March* No. 1 really did 'knock 'em flat' as Elgar had predicted to Dorabella that it would. Henry Wood, the conductor of the Queen's Hall concert in question, never forgot it. 'The people simply rose and yelled. I had to play it again – with the same result; in fact they refused to let me go on with the programme. . . . Merely to restore order, I played the march a third time. And that, I may say, was the one and only time in the history of the Promenade concerts that an orchestral item was accorded a double encore.' The context is significant; Wood and the Queen's Hall manager had founded the Proms in 1895, and *Pomp and Circumstance* No. 1 remains a last-night staple to this day.

Its composer, however, remained a soul divided. On finishing

Cockaigne back in March, he had continued to hark on his impe-
cunious state when he wrote to Richter that 'the work is not tragic
at all – but extremely cheerful like a miserable unsuccessful man
ought to write,' and after conducting *Cockaigne*'s anything but
unsuccessful London premiere in June, he considered a dark
sequel, 'City of Dreadful Night'. The duality was apparent in his
personality. The young Arnold Bax, soon to become a composer
of distinction, visited Birchwood that summer and was surprised
by the meeting: 'hatless, dressed in rough tweeds and riding
boots, his appearance was that of a retired army officer turned
gentleman farmer than an eminent and almost morbidly highly-
strung artist. One almost expected him to sling a gun from his
back and drop a brace of pheasants to the ground . . . he was very
pleasant and communicative in his rumbling voice, yet there was
ever a faint sense of detachment, a hint – very slight, of reserve
and hauteur.' A slightly senior young man who called himself
'Ernest Newman' (his real name was William Roberts) and who
was already making his mark as a music critic, saw a different side:
'he gave me even then the impression of an exceptionally nervous,
self-divided and secretly unhappy man.'

The 'spiritual privacy' that in Newman's view Elgar realized
was coming to an end, found its expression in two exquisite short
works. One was a set of two short pieces revisiting earlier sketches,
composed the following January. The inspiration came from lines
of Lamb, describing receding figures of children who 'are only
what might have been', but the delicacy of feeling that prevents
sentiment from becoming sentimentality in *Dream Children* finds
its truest equivalent in a surprising short story by Rudyard
Kipling, '*They*', about the ghosts of two children (for Kipling, the
inspiration was autobiographical; his elder daughter had died of
pneumonia in 1899). The opportunity for a private pendant to
the two *Pomp and Circumstance* Marches came in the composing of
incidental music for a play by George Moore and W.B. Yeats,
Grania and Diarmid. 'Ireland's greatest love-story,' as Moore called
the legend, embraced the death of the hero, and Elgar was so
touched that for no fee he wrote an understated funeral march,
with another *nobilmente* melody at its heart, a few minutes more
of incidental music and a slip of a song to Yeats' lyrics.

Schuster's success in using his royal connections to secure
Elgar a commission for Edward VII's coronation meant little

compared to the acclaim of the international musical world. That came, thanks to the advocacy of Julius Buths, with two performances of *The Dream of Gerontius* in Germany. The first, at Dusseldorf in December 1901, disproved as far as Elgar was concerned 'the idea fostered at Birmingham that my work is *too difficult*,' for the largely amateur choir was perfect only thanks to painstaking preparation. As for the Gerontius, Ludwig Wüllner, he was 'splendid . . . we never had a singer in England with so much brain.' If the second Dusseldorf performance as part of the Lower Rhine Festival the following May eclipsed the first, that was partly due to the presence of an angelic English contralto, Muriel Foster, and partly to the acclaim of a composer Elgar had heard conducting *Tristan und Isolde* but not met up until now, Richard Strauss. Elgar told Littleton that 'Richard Strauss, who never speechifies if he can help it, made a really noble oration over *Gerontius* . . . & it was worth some years of anguish – now I trust over – to hear him call me Meister!'

By raising his glass to 'the welfare and success of the first English progressivist, Meister Edward Elgar, and of the young progressivist school of English composers', Strauss ruffled the feathers of the musical establishment back in London; but the auspicious alliance was not to be shattered by petty jealousies. Over the next year, Elgar was to become better acquainted with several of Strauss's dazzling tone-poems, notably *Death and Transfiguration* at the Worcester Three Choirs Festival and *Ein Heldenleben* ('A Hero's Life') and *Don Quixote* in London. He was even the unlikely interpreter of the passionate love-scene-cum-finale from Strauss's ribald second opera *Feuersnot* when Henry Wood fell ill before a Queen's Hall concert. For his part, Strauss 'the Wagnershaker', as Elgar called him, conducted *Cockaigne* in Germany and might have taken charge of the long-overdue London premiere of *The Dream of Gerontius* in 1903, had the chorus not clamoured for the composer. The sense of comradeship would survive both World War One and the host of new 'progressivists' that would replace Strauss and Elgar in the vanguard of contemporary music.

Back in London that June, preparations loomed for the first performance of the *Coronation Ode* on the eve of Edward VII's coronation. The big *Pomp and Circumstance* tune had been pressed into service as the Ode's finale (folllowing a 'sneak preview' earlier in the work), originally at the special behest of Clara Butt.

Jaeger had recoiled when he heard the news: 'I say *you will have to* write another tune for the 'Ode' in place of the 'March in D' tune (Trio). I have been trying much to fit words to it; that drop to E . . . & the bigger drop afterwards are quite impossible in singing ANY words to them. They sound downright vulgar: Just try it.' He was right: with any Wembley Stadium crowd or flag-waving last-night Prommers scooping down the intervals on the words 'and glory' and 'mighty', 'downright vulgar' is the only way to describe it. Arthur Benson's original lyrics for the Ode fit uncomfortably, but they still come as a surprise to anyone who knows the more patriotic text. Here there is no mention of bounds being set 'wider still and wider', nor of 'God who made thee mighty'. '*Land of Hope and Glory*' as we understand it was introduced by Clara Butt as a separate song a week before the coronation; the real star of the Ode itself, though the contralto, Louise Kirby Lunn, had a fine reputation, was to be the soprano, Nellie Melba.

The *Coronation Ode* is no mere paean of triumphalism from first to last. Elgar uses his full chorus, orchestra and 36-piece military band with aplomb in the opening movement; but the familiar note of intimacy is sounded by the soprano and tenor in the fourth movement and maintained in the quartet that follows. Royalty had to wait exactly a year to make its own judgement (when the King dozed through most of the piece and sat up with a start as '*Land of Hope and Glory*' began). Only a few days before the ceremony, His Royal Highness was taken ill with appendicitis and the whole thing cancelled. Elgar was not being disingenuous, for once, when he wrote to Jaeger: 'Don't, for heaven's sake, *sympathise* with me – I don't care a tinker's damn! It gives me three blessed sunny days in my own country [i.e., cycling around Malvern] instead of stewing in town. *My* own interest in the thing ceased, as usual, when I had finished the M.S. – since when I have been thinking mighty things.'

'Mighty things', or 'GIGANTIC WORX', as he declared more emphatically on 2 July, were the several parts he had in mind of a vast scheme for the 1903 Birmingham Festival. Thoughts on the scope of it must have been further reinforced by yet another summer visit to Bayreuth, where he saw the first three of Wagner's four *Ring* operas, as well as *Parsifal* (which had left its mark above all on that portion of *The Dream of Gerontius*, the Angel of the Agony's solo, with origins in a theme to depict Judas' guilt).

It would embrace 'the Calling of the Apostles, their Teaching (Schooling) and their Mission, culminating in the establishment of the Church among the Gentiles,' and in its insistence on 'underlying principles' would avoid 'the unnecessary complications of some modern sophistic thought.' Even so, Elgar, who claimed to have been 'selecting the words for many, many years', read voraciously around the subject and consulted learned Anglican clerics. The slightly haphazard zeal of the musician-turned-scholar did not bode well for the ready completion of the task: that December Littleton 'could gather little or nothing from the libretto because it is in such a fragmented state.'

The collection of variant texts became a mania: by February 1903, Dorabella found Elgar's study 'full of Bibles'. On the recommendation of the critic Alfred Kalisch, Elgar visited Rabbi F.L. Cohen, a great authority on Jewish ritual music, who recommended the use of the Shofar or synagogue trumpet to add colour to Elgar's dawn scene in Part One and found him a traditional Hebrew chant for the setting of Psalm 92.

Spectacle and local colour, however, were hardly of the essence in *The Apostles*. Before that vivid sunrise, Christ would be discovered praying on the mountain at night. The pure introspective musical poetry with which Elgar portrayed his spiritual isolation outstripped the Russian artist Kramskoi's vision of the lonely Christ, an engraving that became Elgar's 'ideal' and which he hung in his study. A strange spirituality hovering behind this, and so many other, scenes in *The Apostles* may have had something to do with the death of Elgar's mother in September 1903 (she just missed the triumph of *The Dream of Gerontius* in Worcester Cathedral, albeit shorn of its more Catholic lines). Atmosphere was also imbibed from the lonely setting of Longdon Marsh, discovered on one of Elgar's rural bicycle rides and acknowledged in the score. Yet the most mystical theme of all, a sequence of shifting harmonies going one step further than the string chords of Gerontius' 'strange innermost abandonment' and subsequently labelled 'Christ's Prayer', had been sketched much earlier by Elgar on a Welsh holiday with Rosa Burley – his first by the sea – in 1901, apparently without reference to the 'mighty' work just around the corner. It played an important role in what was to become the final chorus of *The Apostles*, purposefully restrained alongside the 'great blaze' of *Gerontius*'s *'Praise to the Holiest'*, since the disciples only half comprehended the miracle of the Ascension, but even more impressive in scale. The new mysticism of English music, shortly to be taken up by the young Ralph Vaughan Williams, begins here.

Between these two masterly cornerstones of the work, the 'sense of ruin' experienced by Elgar in his most despairing moments was embodied first in 'the great sinner' Mary Magdalene and then, rather more vividly, in Judas, with the saga of the Crucifixion removed to the background. All this cost Elgar bitter moments and a retreat into what some would define as a psychosomatic symptom of a nameless eye disorder throughout the first six months of 1903. At the end of June the composer was forced to admit that the third part, focusing on Peter, would have to be abandoned for Birmingham that year; though the public, as far as George Hope Johnstone of the Festival was concerned, was to assume *The Apostles* a complete work in its own right. Both Richter and the Birmingham Festival Chorus were anxious to make amends for the *Gerontius* fiasco, and although the usual nightmare, hardest on Jaeger, of putting the full score together in time for the performance left Richter with no time for study, and Elgar himself conducted, the chorus covered itself in glory, or at least the veiled glory peculiar to the work, at the first performance on 9 October. The critics sniffed a certain incompleteness, but that in itself lent a special quality to a work described by Jaeger as 'so original, so individual and subjective that it will take the British public ten years to let it soak into its pachydermal mind.'

Another elegiac note was sounded, this time quite unexpectedly, in November, when Alfred Rodewald's sudden death gave Elgar 'the most severe shock that has ever happened to me'. Recent memories of happy times at two of Rodewald's country retreats made it seem still more unreal. The Italian riviera holiday the Elgars now embarked upon took them away from local reminders, but the composer would hardly be able to forget that at the end of it he would return to face the largest gesture his homeland had yet made towards him. This was to be a three-day Elgar festival at Covent Garden in March 1903, initiated by Schuster at Alice's suggestion. Perhaps Elgar hoped that the change of scene would provide him with the inspiration he needed for a new work to crown the festival. It should have been the symphony for Richter, but a large-scale overture for orchestra would have to do. At first he and Alice were jolly even in unpromisingly wet and gray circumstances, but by the time Carice – a companionable age at last – arrived with Rosa Burley in time for Christmas, the dull weather was depressing and uninspiring.

Perhaps the brilliant initial gesture of the Overture *In the South*, a cross between the openings of Strauss's *Don Juan* and *Ein Heldenleben*, was already in place, since its origins as another earlier sketch of bulldog Dan, triumphant after a fight, needed no Italian sunshine to thrive. At last, on the afternoon of 3 January 1904, the sun came out and an expedition to a hillside village called Moglio gave birth to a winsome theme fitted to the words 'Fanny Moglio' for Carice's amusement (in the overture, it first appears on Elgar's favourite pair of clarinets in introspective vein).

Another successful outing to the Vale of Andora, and a typically Italian scene of pines, chapel and shepherd, took the pastoral ideas further; and an awe-inspiring ancient road conjured the massive tread of Roman soldiers. The picture was completed by two emotional ideas: a 'canto popolare', not an Italian folksong but Elgar's own idea, inspired in its simplicity and sung by a solo viola in a tribute to Berlioz's *Harold in Italy*, and the descending steps of another *nobilmente* theme to crown the work even more emphatically than its counterpart in the *Cockaigne* Overture.

In the South made a dazzling finale to the Elgar Festival. The composer conducted, since once again the score was not ready for Richter on time. 'The thing *goes* with tremendous energy and life,' he told Jaeger of rehearsals, humorously brushing off Nimrod's worries that high society would engulf and spoil him. He had rallied from a 'bah, humbug!' rejection of all the court pomp and circumstance – and what the King made of *The Apostles* on the second night of the festival can only be imagined – to a vigorous assertion of the only thing that mattered, the music.

It was only a matter of time, however, before circumstantial honours attended. Honorary degrees over the next eighteen months came from Durham, Leeds, Oxford (Parry's doing), Birmingham and Aberdeen. At the Festival, he was made Freeman of the City of Worcester; William Elgar, now nearly eighty-four, watched the procession from an upper window above the old music shop in the High Street (he died eighteen months later). Most significant of all, Elgar's knighthood was announced in June: 'E. & A. vesy peased & hugged one anosser vesy often,' wrote Alice, in the baby-language common to the times.

He used his influence to argue the case against a Musical Copyright Bill, which would further disempower composers already vulnerable to piracy and exploitation. Better deals with Novellos were imminent, but the *'Enigma' Variations* had only brought him £8 so far and he was 'woefully short of money,' as he told Jaeger in a bleak letter at the end of July in which he threatened to take up teaching the violin again. Still, he and 'the Lady', as she had now become, left Malvern behind for a grander house in Hereford, Plas Gwyn, where they gave their support to the local Conservatives (in January 1906, the Conservative MP for Hereford held his seat; but nationally the party was defeated by the Liberal 'Radicals' Alice found so 'Unspeakable').

The arch-reactionary in the world of music remained Stanford, still 'foaming at the mouth' over Richard Strauss, and resentful, with some justification as it turned out, of the new Professorship of Music offered to Elgar by Birmingham University. Elgar gave the first of six lectures in March 1905. In paraphrasing Strauss's speech at Dusseldorf in 1902, he could not help recalling how Strauss had dared to suggest 'that some Englishmen of later day were not quite so distinguished as Brahms'; and although the speech went on to promote the fostering of 'something broad, noble, chivalrous, healthy and above all, an out-of-door sort of spirit' in British music, and the part Birmingham University might play in helping that, the press inevitably chose to highlight the negative rather than the positive aspects.

Another world-class English score, in the meantime, was already making its mark, namely an *Introduction and Allegro* for the glorious strings of the new London Symphony Orchestra (recently founded by players disenchanted with Henry Wood's refusal to sanction their practice of sending in deputies for his orchestra while they sought more lucrative engagements elsewhere). The simplest idea in the piece dated back to that same Welsh holiday in 1901 that had furnished two themes for *The Apostles*, when Elgar had stood on a cliff 'between blue sea and blue sky' and caught the sound of distant singing. He thought 'perhaps wrongly', that the 'fall of a third' in all the faint melodies he heard might be 'a real Welsh idiom'. In late 1904, similar sounds drifting up to Craeg Lea from the river Wye revived that memory.

Another melody of equal distinction, more restless in mood,

he marked with a quotation from Shakespeare's *Cymbeline* that could apply to so much of his music – 'smiling with a sigh'. The brilliance of the full string effect that Elgar the violinist knew how to conjure was to be served by the full-bodied introduction and what he described to Jaeger as 'a devil of a fugue . . . with all sorts of japes & counterpoint' in place of a conventional central 'working-out' section. The London Symphony strings did the *Introduction and Allegro* full justice not at the first, inadequately rehearsed, performance in March 1905, but on tour to six English cities in November, with Elgar conducting.

Foreign travels that year served first business, then pleasure. His first visit to America was made ostensibly to receive another honorary doctorate at Yale University, initiated by an admiring Professor there, Samuel Sanford – but as with Strauss before him and Mahler after, big bucks for concert appearances were the real draw. No experience on this first trip seems to have encouraged a more informed opinion about Americans than the one made to Jaeger back in 1901 – 'these johnnies only talk-alk-alk-alk-alk-with a blasted twang' – although Elgar did make friends with a charming hostess, Julia Worthington. The visit also bore fruit for an Elgar Festival in Cincinnati the following year, where he conducted his own works before packed, high-paying houses, and a 1907 trip focused around an honorary degree from the Carnegie Institute in Pittsburgh (which ended less than happily when the wealthy Scots-born Andrew Carnegie refused to pay the promised fee which would in Elgar's eyes have made it all worthwhile).

The other voyage of 1905 was a Mediterranean cruise with Frankie Schuster and his aristocratic friends (and without Alice), which showed him the wonders of Istanbul's Bosphorus at sunset and the even more marked exoticism of Smyrna (Izmir), prompting an atmospheric if not markedly oriental-flavoured piano piece. His only other major work of those years for an instrument which interested him little had been the consciously brilliant *Concert Allegro*, composed for the virtuoso Fanny Davies in 1901; *In Smyrna*, striving less hard for effect, achieves the greater impact.

At home, the workload was stressful. More lectures from Birmingham gave him a forum to rail against England's poor track record for solo singers and conductors (the practical conducting course he proposed would not be put into operation until 1919). Then it was time for the more pressing business of the next

Birmingham oratorio, taking up where *The Apostles* had left off. Part of the work was already done: the themes of *The Apostles* would be woven into the fabric as reminiscences along the increasingly elaborate lines of Wagner's later *Ring* operas, to be joined by several new ideas made especially memorable by Elgar as he worked on the fluent Prelude to what would become *The Kingdom* in January 1906. He told Jaeger, addressing him as '*Heart friend*', 'so far it's the best thing I've done *I know*: remember it's not piano music and won't sound well on a tin kettle.'

Then, suddenly, there was another crisis: the outline of the new work's second part failed to materialize and Elgar was all for giving up entirely. Alice saved the situation, offering Littleton at Novellos and Johnstone in Birmingham half the project. As it stood, *The Kingdom* could still work: there was little action, but paradoxically, Elgar would bring it to more robust life than *The Apostles*, where the main events had taken place more or less offstage. As he was eventually able to tell Jaeger, 'the whole thing is intentionally less mystic than the A[postles]: the men are working & the atmosphere is meant to be more direct & simple.'

In March, he worked with a will on the big central scene, where the disciples are 'filled with the spirit' and John delivers an enthusiastic sermon in which Elgar's usual failure to rise to the occasion in the vocal line is offset by the orchestral web of reminiscences. Jaeger had doubts about the big chorus that followed, but Alice fended him off in the belief that the nervous genius could not sustain an 'attack' even from the friend whose advice he valued the most. A long and searching chorus to balance the one at the end of *The Apostles*, in the same noble key of E flat major but with a hint of heroism in the brass, brought the work to a close with the Lord's Prayer, and by 23 July the main task was over, with only the scoring to come. At Birmingham that October, *The Kingdom* followed *The Apostles* as in ideal circumstances it should, given the thematic unity of the two works; although it is *The Kingdom* that many admirers, among them the great Elgar interpreter Sir Adrian Boult, have preferred not just to its predecessor but even to *The Dream of Gerontius*.

The usual depression that descended on Elgar after strenuous creative effort struck harder than ever after the first performance of *The Kingdom*. He gave only two of his Birmingham lectures for the new academic year before leaving at the end of the year for Italy. He did not improve in Naples – 'one thing, I don't want to . . . I am bored to death,' he told Littleton – but Capri raised his spirits and he even took up the violin for high-spirited duets with a mandolin-playing island barber. By the time the Elgars arrived in Rome, he was 'utterly blissful', and the Eternal City was to provide the catalyst for his greatest masterpiece so far when they returned there less than a year later.

The seeds for the masterpiece, which turned out to be the symphony that had been on his mind for nearly a decade, were sown in Hereford during the intervening summer. In the midst of a sudden return to childhood themes in the form of the two *Wand of Youth* Suites, prompted by reflections on his 50th birthday that year and the present of an old family chest sent by his brother Frank, he discovered what Alice called a 'great beautiful tune'. The descending figure with which it began was the final boisterous optimism of the '*Enigma' Variations'* closing bars. There was, too, a certain innate nobility akin to the much more regular *Pomp and Circumstance* tune (another march, with a foursquare melody second only in popular appeal to No.1, had just been completed). Yet its flowing wistfulness linked it to the *Wand of Youth* music and conjured a nostalgic past in much the same way.

Once the symphony was decided upon, and the possibility of a Judgment-day sequel to *The Kingdom* dismissed for the foreseeable future, he took up the great theme that December, surrounded by the hurly-burly of Rome. Its immediate opponent was to be the generator of the first movement's central argument, in a chromatic vein that kept tabs with the progressive musical spirit of the times and at the same time epitomized the profound discontent that so often afflicted the composer. Another restless pattering of semiquavers would suggest the scurry of a hectic world in the scherzo, its pace to be slowed to provide the main theme of a slow movement far removed from outward struggle.

In the meantime, four partsongs for unaccompanied chorus sketched the themes of conflict, withdrawal and victory that characterized the symphony. Since his admiring observation of the choral competitions at Morecambe on the Lancashire coast and the 'real *art* feeling' of the singing there, the partsong had become more than a commercial means to an end. This Op.64 set, with its rarefied harmonies, sudden bursts of confidence and bleak conclusion, enshrined all those poetic virtues he had sensed in the performers. Three of the poems – by Tennyson, Byron and Shelley – were the finest he had set; the fourth, '*Owls*' bore an Italian signature but 'Pietro d'Alba' was in fact a *nom de plume* based on Carice's pet rabbit. The funereal sentiments of the author, effective enough in conjunction with the eerie music, were anything but cuddly.

Would he find a more optimistic ending for the symphony? Creative confidence back home in June was high enough to suggest he might; but the symphonic conflicts were tremendous. Neither a 'sad and delicate' theme nor 'veiled, mysterious' evocations of childhood river magic were strong enough to keep the first-movement monsters at bay, but the *nobilmente* theme would gradually reassert its visionary power in a coda of great subtlety.

The manipulation of themes could only have been practised by a technical master, and Elgar knew it, but he would underplay the complex foundations in his efforts to stress that it all came 'from the heart'. In the Adagio, he set aside the struggle for a profundity of calm expression that Jaeger thought worthy of Beethoven at his finest, and few would disagree; here, the essence of the inner Elgar finds its finest expression. The finale achieved something still more remarkable for a man of his volatile temperament: he carried the *nobilmente* theme through hell and high water in the finale to a genuinely bracing victory so brilliantly scored that there was no hint of vulgar rhetoric.

The finale's main theme of resistance bears an uncanny resemblance to the music of the god Wotan's last conflict with his grandson and representative of a new order, Siegfried, in Wagner's *Ring* opera of that name. Wotan's spear shatters on Siegfried's sword; but Elgar's old order survives, to maintain what he called 'a massive hope in the future'. He never carried it off like that again, but the First Symphony was a watershed in his career, and even then he must have known it. As Hans Richter, 'beloved friend' and dedicatee of the work, prepared its first London performance after the Manchester premiere in December 1908, he said to the players, 'Gentlemen, let us now rehearse the greatest symphony of modern times, *and not only in this country*.' The world was quick to agree with him then, and many of us have come round to believing it now.

CHAPTER 5
RETROSPECTIVES
(1909–17)

The symphony, Elgar was able to tell Schuster's sister Adela on Christmas Day 1908, was 'making a very wild career'. Richter repeated it in London to a packed house, and Elgar conducted the third London performance on 1 January 1909. Public enthusiasm increased. It was hardly his fault if a national mood of increasing belligerence in the years leading up to World War One appropriated his hard-won personal triumph at the end of the symphony; nor that the young conductor Thomas Beecham, when he toured the work with his own orchestra, lopped some twelve minutes' worth of music to arrive at the final victory-charge all the more rapidly. Whatever the misconceptions and the casualties, British audiences were not to feel so sure of a master-piece so close to its conception until Britten's *Peter Grimes* arrived in 1945, at the end of World War Two.

Yet the First Symphony also had the international acclaim it deserved. America was quick on the uptake; in Vienna it was conducted by the Bruckner disciple Ferdinand Löwe and in St Petersburg by Alexander Siloti, who now had the 'great *orchestral work*' he had been waiting for since the '*Enigma*' Variations. Perhaps the most significant advocate of all was Artur Nikisch in Leipzig, who said that if Brahms's First had the nickname of 'Beethoven's Tenth', then this symphony could fairly be called 'Brahms's Fifth'.

Nikisch's approach was possibly even better suited to Elgar's music than Richter's, if one accepts the composer's preference for his works to be performed 'elastically and mystically' rather than 'squarely and sound like a wooden box'. The 20-year-old Adrian Boult made the distinction between Richter and Nikisch in a paper he read to an Oxford University society that same year. He admired Richter's 'steady beat which produces an absolutely even tempo, unbroken sometimes from beginning to end of the longest symphonic movement' but reserved his astonishment for Nikisch's personal magnetism, the way he hypnotized the orchestra and could 'alter the tempo several times in one bar without the slightest loss of ensemble'. The era of the great 'creative' conductor was dawning.

For Elgar, tragedy followed swiftly on triumph's heels. His 'dearest & truest friend' Jaeger died on 18 May 1909. The shock was not, of course, as great as it had been with the sudden loss of Rodewald: Jaeger had been fighting tuberculosis for years, and his continual removal to Davos in Switzerland for rest-cures had left him unable to influence his friend as he would have liked, either musically or in the matter of the wealthy London friends of Elgar's he had eyed so warily. Jaeger's very real suffering before his death failed to encourage a similar fortitude in the depressive Elgar. When Jaeger had told him 'I sometimes wish I *were* dead & had nearly done with all illnesses & worries . . . Never to have a day, *not one* day of a wretched life free from *illness* is awful,' he had far more cause than Elgar, who so often wailed in a similar vein for little outward reason.

At least he could make amends in musical tributes. At the time of Rodewald's death, Jaeger had encouraged him to 'tell us in your music what you dare not say, dare not, because your grief is too deep & great.' He had not done so then, but now there were memorials of all kinds, none of them directly ascribed to Jaeger but all of them reflecting a sense of loss. Staying at a villa in Careggi near Florence, hired by Julia Worthington, he sketched out two partsongs before receiving the bad news that May. One was a simple *Angelus* inspired by the locale, but the words of the other, by the medieval Italian poet Cavalcanti, had massive autobiographical implications: 'Dishevelled and in tears, go, song of mine.' The stricken lament gave way to a characteristically Elgarian largesse in the hope of 'purification'; but his habit, in the partsongs, of returning to the opening lines, made for a desolate ending. Only a sudden flicker from minor to major on the final 'Go!' gave hope for the future. An *Elegy* for strings, commissioned through the agency of Alfred Littleton for a public memorial with which Elgar had no connections, gave him a chance to commemorate his friend in his most personal tones. Yet the greatest laments would resound throughout the four major works to come.

All of them had roots in sketches or plans made long before the *First Symphony*. At the Jaeger Memorial Concert on 24 January 1910, when Richter conducted the '*Enigma*' *Variations*, there were three new songs with orchestra to texts by Gilbert Parker. Interpreted by Elgar's ideal 'angel' Muriel Foster, they struck one critic as 'retrospective in character – the expression of one in whose veins the blood has begun to cool.' The blood could still become heated, but the observation applies in essence to the masterpieces then being conceived. The first, a Violin Concerto, referred back to ideas drafted in 1905 when Elgar had first been encouraged by the great virtuoso who was now to bring the work to life, Fritz Kreisler. Placing Elgar on a level with Brahms and Beethoven, and describing his inspirations as 'pure, unaffected music', Kreisler had then expressed the hope that he would 'write something for the violin.' A concerto had in fact been planned as far back as 1890, but it was only now, in 1910, that Elgar set to work with a will. Between the two ideas of 1905, a bold and dark opening theme and a simple but surprisingly adaptable melody in the vein of the 'Welsh tune' for the *Introduction and Allegro*, he would eventually insert a drooping, melancholy figure which might stand as the signature of a sadder man. He conceived it, he wrote significantly in February 1910, 'in dejection'.

Actual work began in January, however, with the slow movement. Its theme went back further than the original plans for the concerto, and although in the introspective vein of the most withdrawn music for strings in the *First Symphony*, it had more than a hint of placidity about it. The real Elgar would come to the rescue in a single bar of *nobilmente* theme distinguished by a wide, very romantic interval in the phrase; it helped to provide the climax of the movement. London played host to the essential creation of the concerto, begun in Queen Anne's Mansions and resumed in a flat in New Cavendish Street, and Elgar's wife was not always there to fuss over 'the genius'. Another woman played the role not so much of muse as of godmother, and her encouragement helped to fill a gap left by Jaeger.

It was awkward that the Christian name of Alice Stuart-Wortley, daughter of the Pre-Raphaelite artist John Millais and wife of a Sheffield MP in the Schuster 'set', was the same as his wife's. So with playful fancy rather than romantic adoration he called her 'Windflower' after the anemones common to Cornwall, where the Stuart-Wortleys had a summer home, and retrospectively named the first movement's two most soulful themes after the epithet. More serious are the implications of the inscription Elgar chose to head the score, a Spanish motto found in the romance *Gil Blas* which translates 'Herein is enshrined the soul of . . . ' Elgar, with his love of mystification, left the name blank and – ultimately, as he wrote to Nicholas Kilburn – 'indefinite as to sex or rather gender'.

Whatever the nature of the relationship with Alice Stuart-Wortley, about which much fruitless romantic speculation has been made, it was to 'Windflower' that Elgar charted the progress of the work. Schuster, with whom he motored down to the west country that April and whose Thameside 'Hut' figured as a third home for composition, became the other chief confidant, and he soon made it clear to 'Frankie' that news of the death of 'that dear sweet-tempered King Man' on 7 May could not deflect him from spirited creation: 'I have the Concerto well in hand . . . it's *good!* awfully emotional! too emotional but I love it: 1st movement finished & the IIIrd well on – these *are* times for composition.' For all his own skill as a violinist, he was now working with Billy (W.H.) Reed, violinist in the London Symphony Orchestra, on practical details in the solo part, and Reed later described in vivid terms how he found the composer at home surrounded by countless scraps of manuscript.

Mere violinistic effectiveness was left behind as he arrived at the last-movement cadenza. Against a pizzicato thrumming on the strings, the soloist tenderly tried out ideas from previous movements. Sustained at daring length, the cadenza would dissolve the ideas into thin air before reinstating them, and though the thrumming evoked the Aeolian harp-effect Elgar had managed at Plas Gwyn by letting the wind pass through strings fixed to a study window, this was river-magic again – of a kind recently evoked by Elgar's contemporary, Kenneth Grahame. In *The Wind in the Willows*, the Rat and the Mole liken 'the wind playing in the reeds' to 'far-away music . . . the lilting sort that runs on without a stop – but with words in it, too – it passes into words and out of them again – I catch them at intervals – then it is dance-music once more, and nothing but the reeds' soft thin whispering.'

Whether or not the audience at the premiere in November 1910 took such an elusive and personal meditation to its heart, as audiences do today when the performer realizes the special spirit of the cadenza, it expected a triumph at the hands of Kreisler and accepted it as such. Kreisler's interest, however, did not last as long as his enthusiastic statements to the press suggested and there was an unhappy sequel when the world's other leading virtuoso violinist, Eugène Ysaÿe, featured the concerto around the world without the knowledge of Elgar or his publishers, to whom copyright fees were due.

Side by side with the concerto, ideas for another symphony gradually emerged. Here, too, some of the seeds had been sown before the First Symphony took shape, one of them dating from 1904 before *In the South* replaced the projected symphony. The vigour of its leaping dotted rhythms, perfect for the heroism of horns, was intended as a portrait of Richter ('Hans himself'), and the possibility of an heroic symphony was rekindled by hearing Richter rehearse Beethoven's *'Eroica' Symphony* early in October 1909. The similarities between Beethoven's *Third Symphony* and Elgar's *Second* are undeniable: both begin in the horn-brilliant key of E flat major and proceed to a funeral-march second movement in C minor (although Elgar denied that it was a funeral march, and it had nothing to do with world events; Dorabella heard him play it through before the death of Edward VII).

As in the *First Symphony*, the middle movements would set alongside each other the bluster of the outside world (with another theme – 'like something you hear down by the river' – for contrast) and a private gravity. This time, though, the order was reversed, the contrasts extreme rather than connected, and the scherzo would outstrip for sheer raucous terror not only its predecessor but anything that Elgar had composed before. The modern playwright David Pownall, in his play *Elgar's Rondo*, simplifies for dramatic purposes when he suggests that the violence of the movement comes out of nowhere in Elgar's output, for there had been something like it in the upheavals of the previous symphony's first movement and the 'ancient Romans' section of *In the South*. Nor is the movement's central cataclysm an out-of-the-blue vision of world destruction to come, but a climactic return of a wan ghost from the heart of the first movement, where it appears as 'a sort of malign influence wandering thro' the summer night in the garden.' So it was pure autobiography, as he confirmed to orchestral players many years later, when he likened the Rondo climax to 'that dreadful beating that goes on in the brain of a man in high fever'.

The outer portions of the Rondo sound frightening even to modern ears, too, but their innocuous origins lie in a visit to Venice during the Italian holiday of 1909, when his attention was captured in the Piazza San Marco by a group of musicians 'who seemed to take a grave satisfaction in the broken accent of the first four bars.' By the same token, the calm of St Mark's interior inspired first thoughts of the slow movement.

It was not just in occasional nightmares that a more contemporary musical language found a place in the *Second Symphony*. In the *First*, straightforward ideas in the spirit of the nineteenth century had battled it out with chromatic 'modernism' and won in the end. Yet the opening movement of the E flat symphony, though its confident flood of ideas carries all before it in terms of musical argument, soon embraces harmonic complexity and chromatic writing of a shifting, uncertain nature. Elgar would have heard that restless spirit powerfully at work in Strauss's shattering opera *Elektra*, which he had seen at Covent Garden, conducted by Beecham; and although Strauss asserted his own, fundamentally wholesome nature in his next opera, the 'comedy for music' *Der Rosenkavalier*, others would be ready to loosen the bonds of tonality and head towards what the most progressive composer of the younger generation, Arnold Schoenberg, was to look back on as 'the emancipation of dissonance'.

Elgar, like Strauss, was the offspring of an earlier generation and could not turn his back on all he had lived with so easily. So, in the last movement of his symphony, he offered another retrospective and left the nightmares behind. He had taken for his motto lines from Shelley's *Invocation*, 'Rarely, rarely comest thou, Spirit of Delight', and although the symphony, like the poem, had stressed the rarity rather than the manifestation of the spirit itself, the theme associated with the 'Spirit', having launched the work, appeared towards its quiet close in visionary reassurance. Perhaps he was thinking, again, of Richter rather than himself; for the great man announced his retirement from the podium in February 1911, just as Elgar had put the finishing touches of orchestration to his Rondo.

If Richter had left in spirit, so had public enthusiasm for Elgar's music. It remains inexplicable to this day why, so soon after recent acclaim for the other 'mighty works', so few people came to the Queen's Hall for the first performance of the *Second Symphony* on 21 May 1911; and equally inexplicable that those who did, sat through a fine performance conducted by the composer 'like stuffed pigs', as he observed to W.H. Reed afterwards. Not everyone was determined to hail the light and ignore the heart of darkness; Ernest Newman found the Rondo 'terrible in intensity of black import' and summed up: 'Elgar is always saying something fresh. Because an actor has only one voice it does not follow that he can play only one part.'

The actor in question, as usual, declared he was tired of playing any part at all. Just before the *Second Symphony*'s premiere, he went through the motions on a tour to Canada (where he found only 'vulgarity and general horror') and America; and shortly afterwards, the coronation of George V entailed a new movement for the *Coronation Ode* hailing Queen Mary, a rather withdrawn anthem ('*O Hearken Thou*') and a *Coronation March*, which he managed to make more solemn and stern than any of its predecessors. Some unknown and terrible reaction prevented the Elgars from attending the Coronation, which must have pushed Alice's tolerance to the limits, but he did accept an Order of Merit with undisguised pleasure.

By the beginning of the following year, they were Londoners on a grand scale, installed in a large and by all accounts uncomfortable Norman Shaw house in Netherhall Gardens, Hampstead, which Elgar did his best to personalize by re-naming it 'Severn House' (only a plaque to mark the site remains). A luxury billiard table was one of the first new acquisitions, joining his chemical apparatus and microscope as instruments of hobbies he could take seriously, although the social cachet of billiards was more in keeping with the lavish and anything but relaxed entertaining to be done at Severn House.

Yet happiness was not to be found in this latest move: Elgar was unwell again – a doctor diagnosed, falsely as it turned out, Menière's Disease of the middle ear – and Severn House proved expensive to maintain. His new role in following Richter as principal conductor of the London Symphony Orchestra helped a little, though the honour was greater than the financial reward. More lucrative was his first theatre project since *Grania and Diarmid*, incidental music for a 'masque' of the kind so popular at the time, to mark the Indian coronation of the King and Queen, *The Crown of India*. The offer came from the enterprising impresario of the Coliseum Theatre, Oswald Stoll, and it helped Elgar to buy a fine range of second-hand scientific and literary works. He noted the irony of starving for a big work like *Gerontius* and living in relative clover as a result of this 'small effort'; but he carried it out with more care than the 'pageant of empire' subject might suggest, raiding old sketchbooks and scoring dances of alternating delicacy and vividness in a style worthy of the ballet-masters he so admired, Delibes and Massenet.

A weightier task was due for the Birmingham Festival that October. The new work was to sound no festival clarion-call like that of the young Vaughan Williams' *Sea Symphony* at Leeds two years before, a bracing epic indebted to Elgar's example. Back in 1904, Elgar had wanted to set Arthur O'Shaughnessy's poem *The Music Makers*, but by now he had far more material to weave around its theme of art's continuity in the face of 'dreamers of dreams' – his own. The creative artist's loneliness and the encouragement to continue from a friend who 'wrought flame in another man's heart' would be marked respectively by the 'Enigma' theme and 'Nimrod' in its original form, though the setting of the 'flame in another man's heart was to quote the dying fall of the *Second Symphony* (which, he later wrote, was a tribute to Frank Schuster). Other themes of remembrance, woven more subtly than 'Nimrod' into the dream-fabric, came from the *First Symphony*, *Sea Pictures*, *The Dream of Gerontius* and the *Violin Concerto*.

Such self-quotation was hardly new to the late-romantic artist – Strauss had woven a tapestry of his own themes in the 'works of peace' section of *Ein Heldenleben* – but nor was it an excuse for failing inspiration. Elgar asked Ernest Newman, engaged on an analysis for the programme, not to 'insist too much on the *extent* of the quotations, which after all form a very small portion of the work.' He was right, and his two main ideas, echoing the minor and major halves of the 'Enigma' theme, show a strength of invention to rank alongside anything in the *Second Symphony* and the *Violin Concerto*. Perhaps the ambiguity of the message and the usual infelicities of the vocal lines for chorus and contralto prevented *The Music Makers'* special qualities from being appreciated at its first performance. The Birmingham programme on 1 October also featured Sibelius' *Fourth Symphony*, another autobiographical work in which despair gains the upper hand through the starkest of orchestral means; the ode and this symphony must have made a strange pair.

Elgar's perception of the cultural mood of the times surfaces in his refusal to turn back to the third part of *The Apostles* trilogy: 'the whole word is given over to short things – plays & music suffer most.' Surely the real reason was that he had lost his faith. Much as he appreciated the support of Nicholas Kilburn as an encouraging heir to Jaeger – and he showed his appreciation by dedicating *The Music Makers* to Kilburn – he could not accept Kilburn's written attempts at a mystical sort of consolation. 'You say "we must look up?" To what? To whom? Why?' he countered, and continued: 'The mind bold / and independent / The purpose free / Must not think / Must not hope . . . ' adding, by way of identification and comment, 'it seems sad that the only quotation I can find to fit my life comes from the Demons' Chorus [in *The Dream of Gerontius*]! a *fanciful* summing up!!'

The grand setting of Psalm 48 for chorus, organ and orchestra of 1910, with its sunset-glow reflections of the finales to the *Violin Concerto* and *Second Symphony*, was his last strong gesture towards a faith he had left behind; two more anthems followed in 1914, but neither showed any strong personality behind their religious affirmations.

The more than usually sad and rueful Elgar of 1913 is the real character portrayed in his last great symphonic work, a swansong for Leeds. When it was finished, he told Ernest Newman: '*Falstaff* . . . is the name but Shakespeare – the whole of human life – is the theme. A theatre conductor cd easily have given a very heavy scherzo . . . but you will see I have made a larger canvas – & over it all runs – even in the tavern – the undercurrent of our failings and sorrows.' The protagonist this time seemed far removed from the comical aspect of Shakespeare's fat knight, painted in the sombre colours of the orchestra's lower instruments (with cellos playing a major role) and depicted in the 'chromatic harmony and strange blending of keys' that Elgar told a London audience the following year he had long seen as the 'music of the future.'

The music of the age in which he had come to maturity surfaced only in two 'dream interludes' and the confidence of Falstaff's 'boon-companion' Prince Hal. Yet there was ambiguity here, too, for Hal turned militaristic in preparation for his role as Henry V, and would reject the old man at his coronation. Falstaff's memories fragmented into thin air on his death bed and 'the man of stern reality . . . triumphed' in a final, unsettling fanfare.

If this was Elgar's most forward-looking and least predictable score so far, it was also a surprising choice of subject for a composer who had always rejected the more illustrative aspects of Richards Strauss' tone-poems. The 'larger canvas' of *Falstaff* keeps the musical form (in this case symphonic) to the fore, but so, too, does Strauss' *Don Quixote*, in a series of variations more complex, if not more subtle, than Elgar's '*Enigma*' set. Elgar knew his Shakespeare too well not to relish such sketches as the incident of Falstaff's duping in the Gadshill exploit, or his drunken speeches in the tavern at Eastcheap (a splendid role for the solo bassoon, more graphic than the wistful *Romance* Elgar had written for the instrument three years earlier). He gleaned the incidents from *Henry IV Parts One and Two* and Mistress Quickly's narrative of Falstaff's death in *Henry V*, rejecting the roustabout of *The Merry Wives of Windsor* – unlike Boito, who fused comedy and history plays for Verdi's sparkling opera, *Falstaff*. Like Verdi, Elgar toyed with another Shakespearean subject as a possible opera – *King Lear*; for he had just met the ideal interpreter in the great Russian bass Fyodor Chaliapin. The project was surely doomed to founder, for the idea of an Elgar *King Lear* seems unimaginable in a way that an Elgar *Return of the Native* or *The Woodlanders*, two Hardy adaptations proposed by Sidney Colvin at the same time, do not.

As it happened, *Falstaff* was to stand alone as Elgar's opera not for voices but for orchestra. Again audiences, disconcerted by the sombre tone, failed to recognize it as a masterpiece either at Leeds in October 1913 or in London the following month. The conductor Landon Ronald valiantly championed three performances, but only the third drew a decent crowd. Ronald had better tidings for Elgar in the New Year: gauging correctly his curiosity in scientific matters, he introduced Elgar to a representative from the Gramophone Society. The result was an agreement with a publisher of light music for two new pieces, with substantial composer's royalties from 'mechanical instrument reproduction'.

The history of the gramophone was still in its primitive early days, when only a relative minority of orchestral players could be crowded round an acoustic horn. One of the new pieces, *Carissima*, was a suitably intimate case for such treatment, and still sounds well in Elgar's performance; but his recording of the *Pomp and Circumstance March* No.1 a few months later points up the short-comings of a much-reduced orchestra, as well as a slimmed-down version of the march, focusing on the big tune, to fit on on side of a 78-r.p.m. record. The style of the string playing, with slides from note to note known as *portamento*, sounds bizarre to us now, but was common at the time.

The second piece, *Sospiri*, turned out to be much too serious for its light-music brief – its place was eventually taken by the 1882 *Douce pensée*, revised as *Rosemary* – and stands as another elegy still awaiting wider popularity with a public fond of string laments like Barber's *Adagio*. Other shorter pieces of 1914 proved both lucrative and heartfelt; choral groups still clamoured for partsongs, but Elgar, for his part, still saw them as vehicles for deeper expression. One of two settings of the fine seventeenth-century poet Henry Vaughan, *The Shower*, expresses in powerful musical terms the hope that 'My God would give a sunshine after rain'; and the 'biggest', as Elgar wrote, of three responses to Russian poets in translations by Rosa Newmarch, is a gloomy vision of '*Death on the Hills*' – as sombre in its ghostly refrains as the first part of the 1909 Bret Harte setting *The Reveille*.

This, rather than the personal nightmares in the Second Symphony, was the real prophecy of things to come. War broke out in August 1914, while the Elgars were on holiday in north-west Scotland. At first, Elgar's sentiments were as conventional as those of most other people: 'the spirit of the men is splendid'; 'the times are spacious & we must win through'; 'I am going to die a Man if not a musician' (too old to fight, he was accepted as a special constable for Hampstead). He was more convinced than his poet, the thoughtful Arthur Benson, of the need to add a vengeful stanza to '*Land of Hope and Glory*'. Yet his famous remark to Schuster that 'the men and women can go to hell – but my horses; – I walk round & round this room cursing God for allowing dumb brutes to be tortured' was made in late August, before the toll of war began to rise to hundreds of thousands of lives.

By December 1915, the losses of 'plucky little Belgium' at Louvain, Liège, Malines and countless other cities could still be offset against the will to fight back, with a stalwart four-note peal of bells in *Carillon*, for reciter and orchestra. Tita Brand Cammaerts, wife of the Belgian who had written the stirring lyrics, recited at the first performance, with Elgar conducting, and the work crested along, in every conceivable arrangement, on the wave of public enthusiasm; in January 1915, Elgar's recording of an abridged version with the actor Henry Ainley sold well.

Yet the implications of the countless deaths in the trenches cried out for stronger commemoration. Grief might be 'glorified & lifted up & transformed,' as the poet Laurence Binyon wrote to Elgar in March, but it also had to be respected. Binyon was writing to encourage Elgar in his plan to set three of his poems from a collection called *The Winnowing Fan* – a plan that looked like faltering when Elgar learned that the young composer Cyril Rootham was setting the same words (Rootham's version went ahead and was published, but so – eventually – did Elgar's, to Rootham's petty-minded resentment). Elgar 'glorified & lifted up' 'the spirit of England, ardent-eyed' in his first setting, but the second movement, '*To Women*', sustained a more desolate note and the third, '*For the Fallen*' took that desolation to greater heights. Light flickered in a disconcertingly jaunty march for the soldiers who 'went with songs to the battle' and a great, emotional climax, but 'For the Fallen' began and ended in shadow; and at Binyon's most famous commemorative lines, 'they shall grow not old, as we that are left grow old. . . . We will remember them,' Elgar inserted an oboe phrase epitomizing the bewilderment of the bereaved.

'*For the Fallen*' was the twentieth century's first great war requiem, to be followed by Vaughan Williams' *Dona nobis pacem* in 1936 and Britten's *War Requiem* of 1961, blending the Latin mass for the dead and Wilfred Owen's poems from the trenches. Britten set finer poetry than Elgar, but in 1915, Binyon's sentiments still counted for something. 'Sketched and nearly completed' by the end of Spring 1915, the last two of the three settings that make up *The Spirit of England* were not performed until nearly a year later, when the need for them was even greater. 'The Fourth of August' only joined them in 1917, after Elgar finally decided to set Binyon's stanza about Germany as 'vampire of Europe's wasted will', with music from the Demons' Chorus of Gerontius. 'Two years ago,' he told Ernest Newman, 'I held over that section hoping that some trace of manly spirit would show itself in the direction of German affairs; that hope is gone forever & the Hun is branded as less than a beast for very many generations.'

Dramatic entertainment's part in the war effort for 1915 turned Elgar temporarily into a man of the theatre. Carillon was dressed up to run at the Coliseum in August. Following a 'Fantasia on Polish themes', Polonia, to help raise funds for the war on the eastern front, Elgar set another Cammaerts poem, Une Voix dans le désert, which ended up sharing an unlikely triple bill at the Shaftesbury Theatre with Leoncavallo's Pagliacci and Mascagni's Cavalleria Rusticana (which the conservative Elgar had so disliked for its portrayal of 'low life' when he first saw it in 1891).

A third Cammaerts setting, Le Drapeau belge, missed the wave of popular support for Belgium when British sympathies became absorbed in larger war concerns. Elgar's last project for 1915 was actually tailor-made for the theatre. The opportunity it offered for escapism must have come as a welcome relief, the more so since the play for which Elgar was to provide the incidental music, an adaptation of Algernon Blackwood's novel A Prisoner in Fairyland, mirrored with uncanny precision the themes of his own childhood play. Blackwood's children, like the young Elgar's, knew the way to a magical, starlit realm that 'wumbled' adults, out of touch with their emotions, had lost. It was no coincidence that the play version of Peter Pan was running successfully at another London theatre: the theme of hard fact versus delicate fantasy was more popular than ever in the early years of the war.

The hour and twenty minutes of music Elgar provided for The Starlight Express, as the play was called, inevitably drew on The Wand of Youth Suites, but – as with The Music Makers – fine new invention perfectly complemented the old ideas. This was no harbinger of a Lloyd-Webber extravaganza: the text may have been 'preachy and pretentious', but the music played its part, as one critic observed, 'very subtly and yet very simply.' The 'pagan' designs for the Kingsway Theatre production by the Arts and Crafts President Harry Wilson horrified Blackwood and Elgar, who wrote that Wilson was an 'ignorant silly crank' who 'ought to be put in a Home!' Yet this did not stop him from going to gape at the show in childlike wonder as often as he could during its month-long run. After that, there was the gramophone to keep extracts from this favourite child alive. The soprano for the recording was Agnes Nicholls, who had made such an impact in *The Kingdom* and would go on to master the taxing soprano part of *The Spirit of England*, and the baritone, the young Charles Mott, had already become one of Elgar's great white hopes as an interpreter as well as a firm friend. He had played one of the leading 'figures of fancy', the Organ Grinder, in the production of *The Starlight Express*, and in 1917 he went on to take the lead role in a far less delicate wartime production of Elgar's, *The Fringes of the Fleet*. Kipling's verses, which the poet (with his son reported missing in action) was reluctant to entrust to foursquare music, described the wartime uses to which small vessels had been put, and in the tremendously successful Coliseum staging, Mott and his three fellow baritones wore boots and sou'westers.

An extended run for *The Fringes of the Fleet* gave Mott an extended leave of absence from the trenches. Yet return could not be delayed for ever. Mott wrote to Elgar from France in May 1918:

> There is something very much wrong with a world that still sanctions war & something wrong with our practice of the various forms of religion too. . . . O, what a golden opportunity awaits everyone who cares to think at all. You, my dear Sir Edward, realised this years before the war commenced. What consolation to recall your glorious Gerontius & that beloved work 'To the Fallen'. I shall be thinking a great deal of both works & have been of late.
>
> There is one thing that 'puts the wind up me' very badly & that is of my being wiped out & thus miss the dear harmonies of your wonderful works. . . . But I have a supreme confidence in my destiny & feel that I have some useful work to do in the world before I am called away.

The letter must have dealt a final blow to Elgar's own faltering confidence in 'higher powers'. Only hours after writing it, Charles Mott was killed in action.

CHAPTER 6
A KNIGHT OF GHOSTS AND SHADOWS
(1917–34)

- ♦ *Sussex idyll*
- ♦ *Cello Concerto*
- ♦ *Life after Alice*
- ♦ *An opera and a symphony*
- ♦ *Quiet curtain*

As the horrors of the World War One escalated, Elgar lavished what little escapism he could afford in musical terms on *The Starlight Express* and another, slighter piece of dramatic whimsy for a charity matinée ballet *The Sanguine Fan* (the fan in question depicted classical and Watteauesque figures in a woodland scene, brought to life by the modest 'choreography'). There were still viable retreats in the real world, too. Visits to his sister Pollie's family in the country at Stoke he kept to himself; Alice never came, either because her husband did not want her to or because Lady Elgar's long-preserved class values kept her at bay. Yet it was very much at her initiation that a last summer idyll that would outlive the war began, not in Worcestershire but in Sussex, close enough for the ageing composer to fulfil his London engagements without undue stress of travel.

Reconnaissance was made in May 1917. The place, Brinkwells at Fittleworth, gave a distant view of the river Arun, to remind Elgar of the Severn and the Wye, and recalled the lost idyll of Birchwood, with its cottage and its woods (a similar fate befell the trees of both places, chopped down before Elgar had properly made his farewells). They spent all too little time there in the remainder of 1917 before Elgar's long-term illness turned out to be not the dreaded Menière's Disease but severe tonsillitis and he underwent an operation in London the following March. Yet Brinkwells was to serve as fertile soil for the development of new ideas drafted that month on his return from the hospital to Severn House: a lonely E minor theme destined for his last concerto, and several disconsolate figures for a string quartet. This was a medium he had considered in his youth and again in 1907, when the sketches he made for the Brodsky Quartet went into the *First Symphony*. The nearest he had come was the magnificent *Introduction and Allegro* for strings, pitting a solo quartet against the full string orchestra; and something of that work's mobile spirit crystallized in a new, elliptical form as he worked on the *String Quartet*. If one theme in the *Introduction and Allegro* had seemed perfectly suited to the *Cymbeline* quotation 'smiling with a sigh', so much of the quartet would seem to be sighing with only the passing hint of a smile. That included the slow movement, in which Alice found 'captured sunshine' but which only begins in consolatory vein before fragmenting into laments.

Two other chamber works in fact intervened before the completion of the *String Quartet* at Brinkwells in late 1918. That July he began a *Violin Sonata*, interrupting composition for pleasurable labours of a different sort: carpentry and fishing. He found a monosyllabic companion in his woodwork, a local man called Mark Holden; and, pained as Mark may have been by his master's efforts, Elgar was no *poseur* in the role of woodman-cooper. W.H. Reed arrived at Brinkwells in August to play through the sonata, and perceiving on the skyline 'a tall woodman leaning a little forward upon an axe with a very long handle,' he soon realized it was Elgar. 'He did these things without knowing it, by pure instinct,' Reed added.

It was the Birchwood existence raised to a rare degree of perfectionism; but there were stark ghosts in these woods, too. A group of dead trees stood on a knoll above Brinkwells called Bedham; they made 'a ghastly sight in the evening,' as Reed thought, with their gnarled and twisted branches like supplicating arms. Elgar was fond of ghost stories, and it appears that Algernon Blackwood, who paid a visit to Brinkwells, embroidered a local legend to suit him: these could only be the dead forms of a group of Spanish monks, struck dead while carrying out impious rites. There had indeed been mendicant monks in Sussex, but they were certainly not Spanish. The flavour, however, suited Elgar, who was able to introduce into his new *Piano Quintet*, the *Violin Sonata*'s successor, an eerie dance with a Spanish-Moorish flavour. He began the quintet with muttered chants from the strings against a sustained line in the piano, and followed it with a sigh for the strings both ghostly and at the same time characteristic of his own more depressed moments. The monks' evil influence extends, according to Reed, to the weird atmosphere of the *Violin Sonata*'s slow movement.

Yet despite the new ghostly note both the *Piano Quintet* and the *Violin Sonata*, spare though it is in a way that could only have been achieved by a composer who knew the instrument's more subtle potential, look backwards to an earlier influence. It is not just the sometimes fulsome piano parts that conjure Brahms: several of the ideas in the Quintet's first movement and the opening statement of the finale could have been written by that composer, although Elgar extends his range around his Brahmsian subjects.

Perhaps he was harking back again, as in the *Second Symphony*, to the virtues of 'Hans himself'; for Richter, who had saddened his English friends by handing back British honours shortly after the start of the First World War and who died in 1916, was much on his mind 'while I am working with the hoe and plane'. He confided that to another dear German friend, Mrs. Marie Joshua, and it was to her that he offered the dedication of the *Violin Sonata*. 'I fear it does not carry us any further,' he told her, 'but it is full of golden sounds and I like it . . . you must not expect anything violently chromatic or cubist.' Her sudden death before she could decide whether or not to accept the honour led Elgar to recast the sonata, incorporating the long melody that finally takes wing in the slow movement as what Alice called 'a wonderful soft lament' in the finale.

Alice herself was far from well, and Elgar did not realize the seriousness of her condition when he saw unwelcome visits to London to see the doctor and for an operation only as 'a *tragedy* for my music'. But piecemeal work on the *Piano Quintet* and the *String Quartet* did finally reach completion. A final flourish that was to become the best-loved of all his works grew from the first stirrings of fresh creativity – the 'orchestral' E minor theme of

1918. Now, fifteen months later, with the three chamber works successfully premiered or previewed by friends and colleagues, he found himself back at Brinkwells 'frantically busy' on 'a Concerto for Violoncello – a real large work & I think *good* & alive.' The end result was to be more sombre than he suggested. When the Armistice finally arrived the previous November, Binyon had asked him to set his 'Peace Ode' to music, and Elgar had replied that 'the whole atmosphere [of the time] is too full of complexities for me to feel music to it.' Another requiem was more in order; and one idea for the *Cello Concerto* Alice had already noted as 'another lament wh. shd. be in a war symphony.'

The very nature of the cello, requiring orchestral restraint above and beneath the instrument's register in order to allow it to project, bound it to an introspective mode. Only briefly, in the finale, did Elgar allow soloist and orchestra to behave *nobilmente* – the once-favourite marking that surfaces only very briefly in Quintet and Quartet – and boisterously, like *The Wand of Youth*'s wild bears and giants. Otherwise, here was a slimmed-down Falstaff at his most ruminative: another self-portrait, in other words. The music moved into a major key, very wistfully, only at the heart of the first movement before flying off into a *scherzo* dream interlude and cautiously revealing its tender soul in a brief but telling *Adagio*, the quintessence of what Ernest Newman at the first performance called 'that pregnant simplicity that has come upon Elgar's music in the last couple of years.' The last reminiscences of that *Adagio* towards the end of the piece re-enacted the cadenza of the *Violin Concerto*, but with the terseness that characterizes the concerto as a whole.

The first performance on 27 October 1919 faltered not because of the soloist, Felix Salmond, who arrived with the Elgar seal of approval, but because of the London Symphony Orchestra's new principal conductor, the often inspirational Albert Coates, who had simply spent too much rehearsal time on his beloved Wagner and far too little on the concerto (the first of two recordings, with the graceful Beatrice Harrison, was a compromise, too, cut to fit the 78-r.p.m. sides). A happier event was the triumphant reinstatement of the *Second Symphony* by the young Adrian Boult the following March. Elgar's words cast us forward as far as 1976, when the 86-year-old Boult completed his last recording of the symphony, one of recorded history's great glories:

'With the sounds ringing in my ears I send a word of thanks for your splendid conducting of the Sym: – I am most grateful to you for your affectionate care of it & I feel that my reputation in the future is safe in your hands. It was a wonderful series of sounds. Bless you!' Alice, characteristically, doubled the thanks to Boult: 'I know you will like to hear that Edward was *so* happy & delighted – it has done him so much good.'

It was the last performance Alice attended. She died of the cancer that the doctor had only belatedly recognized on the evening of 7 April, in her husband's arms. At the funeral, W.H. Reed and his colleagues played the *Piacevole* slow movement from the *String Quartet* she had loved so much; Elgar asked Sir Henry Wood if he 'could some day play my wife's favourite movement *by* [read *with*] *all your strings.*' Alice was buried in the churchyard of the Roman Catholic St Wulstan's just beneath the Malvern Hills; Elgar wanted 'the NEXT SPACE to the little lonely occupied grave,' and his old friend from the *Variations*, Troyte, made the arrangements.

The implications of 'a past gone. shattered' were enormous, and Rosa Burley erred on the uncharitable side in stressing the element of guilt that Elgar might have felt. The couple had indeed spent more time apart in later years, and friends had always noticed his gruff impatience with many of Alice's blander gushings. What this extraordinary marriage really meant, though, no one will ever have a right to say, for Elgar eventually destroyed all the correspondence between them that might have given the deepest key to understanding. The one certainty is that Alice found her genius when no one else was prepared to recognize him, and nurtured him as she thought best.

Only days after the funeral he found himself 'plunged in the midst of ancient hate & prejudice – poor dear A.'s settlements and her *awful aunts* who wd. allow nothing to descend to any offspring of *mine* – I had forgotten all the petty bitterness but I feel just now rather evil that a noble (& almost brilliant) woman like my Carice should be penalised by a wretched lot of old incompetents simply because I was – well – I.' Carice proved a tower of strength in her own quiet, intelligent way. The following year, having lost the man she might have married in the First World War, she accepted the proposal of a Surrey farmer, Samuel Blake, with her father's blessing, but although they moved away she remained a good and loyal daughter to the end.

Severn House proved impossible to run in the austerity of the post-war years, and soon went up for auction. Another summer at Brinkwells, so much associated with Alice, only made Elgar sadder and lonelier – the more so when the woods he loved were felled. He wrote to Sidney Colvin: 'Inscrutable nature goes on just the same . . . but I miss the little, gentlest presence & I cannot go on.' The phrase has been taken at long-term face value, as if with Alice's death the wellspring of creation dried up in the last thirteen years of Elgar's life. It was certainly to surface more fitfully; but he remained the same, changeable figure prone to pronounce his music gone forever. Arthur Thomson, the doctor who treated him in 1925 after an operation for haemorrhoids, gauged him correctly: 'again and again he would come in depressed, as if all useful life was over; and after reassurance, he would brighten up perfectly.'

The brightening in the early 1920s took longer than usual, due to the severity of the bereavement; but it was a big step from 'Music I loathe – I did get out some paper – but it's all dead' to declaring: 'Now that my poor wife has gone I can't be original, and so I depend on people like John [sic] Sebastian for a source of inspiration.' He decided to orchestrate one of the Bach fugues he had played through all those years ago, the C minor; the result was perhaps the most brilliant and dazzling Bach transcription of them all. He told Ernest Newman in October 1921, preparing for the Queen's Hall premiere under Eugene Goossens, 'you will see that I have kept it quite solid (diapasony) at first; – later you hear the sesquialteras & other trimming stops reverberating & the resultant vibrating shimmering sort of organ sound – I *think*.'

Movingly reunited with his old friend Strauss, 'Richard the Lion-heart' as he still referred to him, at a lunch-party for young British composers the following January, he discussed with him the orchestration of Bach's organ music. Strauss was true to the principles of his own tributes to music of an earlier age in preferring more restraint. It is a pity he never sealed a new Anglo-German collaboration with a promised orchestration of the *C minor Fugue*'s preceding *Fantasia*; Elgar ended up completing the job himself, the relative austerity of the arrangement perhaps taking to heart Strauss's opinion. Another full-blooded transcription, of the Handel *Chandos Overture in D minor* he had known as a boy and loved for its epic quality, followed in 1923.

The memory of Alice finally led him to some powerfully original creative work. He told the poet of *The Spirit of England* it was because 'my wife loved your things' that he would try to furnish linking music to the scenes of Binyon's *King Arthur*, staged at the Old Vic in March 1923. The score he provided was for a pit orchestra consisting of a mere ten players, which he further undertook to conduct himself. Yet not only did he come up with music of real distinction for a banquet and a battle, but he touched a new vein for the sombre nobility of King Arthur and Sir Bedivere – ideas full of symphonic potential, as he was to realize at the end of his life. The final grave depiction of Arthur and his court on their way to Avalon marching 'mistily past' might have been an elegy for Alice.

Its mood was resumed in two partsongs for male voices. '*The Wanderer*', roaming the woodlands in a poem by an unknown author, was himself, and he fitted equally well the description of the 'knight of ghosts and shadows' with whom the wanderer was to 'tourney'. A second ghostly song seemed to glorify British valour in the First World War, and the sentiments were Elgar's own (under the pseudonym of 'Richard Mardon'). The autobiographical note of lament was resumed in two further partsongs, one setting Walter de la Mare's *The Prince of Sleep*, the other culminating in a bloodcurdling cry of Death claiming the soul of an old king.

It was not all sadness and grief in those later years. A journey up the Amazon in late 1923 must have opened new horizons, though what they were a curious lack of documentation leaves us to guess; James Hamilton Paterson has done just that in *Gerontius*, a fictionalized portrait of the composer that movingly takes the full measure of his complexity. Leasing a house in Kempsey south of Worcester, Elgar declared to Ernest Newman: 'In my own land I am a boy again' (he finally settled at last in Worcester, in a house called Marl Bank). A succession of dogs – Juno, Marco, Mina – became his best friends, recalling the consolations of a bleak time in his youth when 'Scap', a present from the Bucks, helped to mend a broken heart. He noted Whitman's famous lines beginning 'I think I could turn and live with animals, they are so placid and self-contain'd' and quoted them in a Christmas greeting. The human scene offered a mixture of pleasure and pain. He was bewildered by the post-war world of jazz bands and 'waitresses with *very short skirts*', and found a 'Pageant of Empire' with his own music at Wembley Stadium, complete with amplifiers and aeroplanes, 'all mechanical and horrible – no soul and no romance'.

Yet he could use the new improvements in mechanical reproduction to commit vital interpretations to disc uncompromised. The advent of the electric microphone banished the unsatisfactory arrangement of musicians huddled round a horn. In 1927, Elgar conducted a performance of *The Dream of Gerontius* in the Royal Albert Hall which could be relayed to engineers of what was now His Master's Voice in the New Queen's Hall. Only portions of the great work could be recorded, but Elgar's account of his own Prelude before an unusually bronchitic audience still comes across as one of the greatest examples of finely-sculpted conducting.

Even in old age, though, he was still far from aggrandizing his own music. The readings of his two finest successors in the field of interpretation, Sir John Barbirolli and Sir Adrian Boult, slowed down in later years, and not necessarily to detrimental effect; and yet Elgar's second version of his *Second Symphony* is remarkably febrile and volatile. His recordings after that went from strength to strength: Fred Gaisberg of His Master's Voice was wise enough to realize the necessity for the composer to leave behind a recorded legacy. Had Elgar done nothing else in his final years, it would have been enough. Still, the success of his music remained uncertain: more official honours, including a baronetcy and the post of Master of the King's Musick which he took on to save it from extinction, still conflicted with popular neglect.

Schuster died in June 1928, 'five days after Elgar's 75th birthday: he left behind 'highest & sweetest' memories as well as £7,000 to the man 'who has saved my country from the reproach of having produced no composer worthy to rank with the Great Masters.' Elgar had less need to take on any commissions that paid reasonably well, but he managed one to fulfil a long-promised obligation to a music editor, Herbert Whiteley, who wanted an Elgar work for the 1930 Brass Band Competition Festival at the Crystal Palace. He raided old sketches for a *Severn Suite*, and when he refurbished the work for orchestra two years later, the work's dedicatee, George Bernard Shaw was amazed by the 'transfiguration' – 'nobody will ever believe that it began as a cornet corobbery. It's extraordinarily beautiful.' That was especially true of the Fugue, which he subtitled 'Cathedral' (Worcester Cathedral, of course). It might have been made for the strings which now launched a last, noble slow movement. There is no compromise, either, in the *Nursery Suite* dedicated in 1930 to the Princesses Margaret and Elizabeth (and – a nice touch – recorded in the presence of the Duke and Duchess of York and the Princess Elizabeth before the official first performance). Like the *Wand of Youth* suites over two decades earlier, it had been suggested by an old trunk full of childhood sketches, and its miniatures were the *Wand of Youth*'s equals. This time, though, there was a more nostalgic epilogue in which Elgar the solo violinist summoned up memories in the manner of the *Violin Concerto*'s cadenza.

The grand old man to whom the *Severn Suite* was dedicated had turned into Elgar's staunchest supporter. In 1904 Elgar had thought the Shaw of *Man and Superman* 'hopelessly wrong . . . on fundamental things' and 'an amusing liar'. By the 1920s, Elgar, the dyed-in-the-wool Tory, still found Shaw's politics 'appalling' but told Sidney Colvin 'he is the kindest-hearted, gentlest man I have met outside the charmed circle,' and it does Elgar credit that he was curious enough to read *The Intelligent Woman's Guide to Socialism and Capitalism* when Shaw sent him a copy fresh off the press in 1928. For his part, Shaw – who in his early days had been a colourful music critic under the pen-name of 'Corno di bassetto' – never doubted Elgar's place in 'carrying on Beethoven's business' and was disgusted by England's lack of pride in 'one of the greatest composers in the world.'

He was persistent in urging Elgar towards a new orchestral work, asking him once he had finished *The Apple Cart* in 1929 to 'clap it with a symphony'. There was a brief stirring, but then Elgar went ahead with the very thing that Shaw had warned against – an opera. Nor was his choice of subject, Ben Jonson's *The Devil is an Ass*, a suitable one. Like Richard Strauss, news of whose dramatization of Jonson's *Epicœne* as *Die schweigsame Frau* in 1933 may have put a stop to Elgar's plans, his temperament tended too much towards the sentimental (in the positive sense of the word) to respond adequately to Jonson's scabrous, cynical portrait of corrupt society. Even though Alice was no longer there to voice prim censure, as she had been when Elgar portrayed the

Eastcheap woman so tamely in *Falstaff*, there was not to be the slightest hint of naughtiness in this project. Percy Young's realization of Elgar's sketches for *The Spanish Lady*, as the opera was to be called, suggests Elgar's usual inadequacy of vocal setting as well as a failure to characterize individuals in musical terms, so essential to a true man of the theatre. Only the dances, mere pastiches of a vanished age and capped by a spirited *Bolero*, hint at a creative spark.

There is, then, no need to mourn the demise of *The Spanish Lady*. A potential *Third Symphony*, however, presents a different case altogether. Shaw provided very practical fuel for the fire, which flickered throughout the summer of 1932. He wrote to the Director General of the BBC, Sir John Reith, asking him in eloquent terms to commission the symphony, and a date was eventually fixed for a performance in May 1934. There can be no doubt that Elgar's imagination was engaged in the project; only illness and death put a stop to it. From the surviving sketches, a few of them fully scored and the rest written for piano, and from W.H. Reed's vivid description of playing over the ideas with Elgar, we can glean a good sense of 'what might have been'.

The symphony was to be less epic in scope than either of its predecessors, closer to the so-called 'neo-classical' spirit of the times, with several substantial passages carrying repeat marks. The opening, based on a sketch for the never-to-be-completed Judgment Day oratorio to follow *The Apostles* and *The Kingdom*, exists in full orchestration. It evokes a strange world, its bare intervals suggesting the leaner musical language of the German composer Hindemith then at the forefront of new music. Elgar reveals his old self with a second theme (for piano only) close to earlier, wistful second subjects; this one was inspired by his romantic friendship with a young violinist, Vera Hockman, and bears her name (another collaboration with an attractive string player, Jelly d'Arányi, has provided sketchier food for recent speculation).

A gracious interlude was to take the place of a scherzo, carrying over music from the Banqueting Scene of *King Arthur* virtually unaltered but also featuring a new Elgarian inspiration of supreme delicacy as its second episode. Arthur and Sir Bedivere were pressed into service for the finale, but little is known of how it might have ended: perhaps with a reminiscence from the slow movement. This contained Elgar's starkest new music, and he knew it, telling Ernest Newman: 'I am fond enough to believe that the first two bars ... open some vast bronze doors into something strangely unfamiliar.'

As his biographer Basil Maine put it, the air was certainly 'full of harsh conflict'. 'I am in a maze regarding events in Germany – what are they doing?' he asked Adela Schuster in March 1933. 'The Jews have always been my best & kindest friends – the pain of these news is unbearable & I do not know what it really means.' He was still able to play his part in central European civilization as he knew and understood it, making his first flight to Paris at the end of May to conduct the *Violin Concerto* with Yehudi Menuhin, the 17-year-old prodigy with whom he had already recorded the work.

He found time to pay a visit to the blind and paralysed Delius at Grez-sur-Loing. Delius, who was to outlive Elgar only by a few months, had conveyed his sense of the ineffable in musical terms very differently, but shared Elgar's exquisite delicacy of expression. He asked Elgar what flying was like and Elgar recalled:

> *'Well,' I answered, 'to put it poetically, it is not unlike your life and my life. The rising from the ground was a little difficult; you cannot tell exactly how you are going to stand it. When once you have reached the heights it is very different. There is a delightful feeling of elation in sailing through gold and silver clouds. It is, Delius, rather like your music – a little intangible sometimes, but always very beautiful. I should have liked to stay there for ever. The descent is like our old age – peaceful, even serene.'*

Serenity was temporarily shattered when in October an attack of what he thought to be the sciatica that had so troubled him led to an operation; and the operation revealed inoperable cancer. Doctor Thomson was an admiring chronicler of his fortitude: 'after all his years of worrying over imagined troubles, he displayed magnificent courage in the face of great adversity.' He told the doctor 'he had no faith whatever in an afterlife' and added 'If I can't complete the *Third Symphony*, somebody will complete it – or write a better one – in fifty or five hundred years. Viewed from the point where I am now, on the brink of eternity, that's a mere moment in time.' Some of the old ghosts returned to haunt him, for he told Ernest Newman on his deathbed something which, Newman said, 'I have never disclosed to anyone and have no intention of ever disclosing. . . . ' Could it have been so terrible that Newman had to carry the secret to his grave – or was it simply another statement of his lost faith?

At any rate nature, rather than religion, had all the last words. In January, Elgar supervised a recording by telephone from his bedroom. Lawrance Collingwood and the London Symphony Orchestra played first the *Triumphal March* and then the Woodland Interlude from *Caractacus* – that very piece that he had quoted when he wrote to Jaeger 'the trees are singing my music – or have I sung theirs?' The deeply Catholic son of Hubert Leicester was shocked to hear him ask for his cremated ashes to be scattered at the confluence of the rivers Severn and Teme, and assumed he was 'off his head with morphia'; but he was no doubt in earnest. On the morning of 23 February, as Carice put it, 'he just slept away.'

He was buried beside Alice in the cemetery below the hills – not far from the rivers, and surrounded by the trees that he had faithfully reflected in the introspective moments that are the real heart and soul of his music.

EDWARD ELGAR: COMPLETE LIST OF WORKS

ORIGINAL WORKS

c.1867   Music for a children's play, twice revised and eventually used in *The Wand of Youth* Suites (see also 1907)

c.1870   *Fugue in G minor* for organ (unfinished)

c.1872   *O salutaris hostia* for unaccompanied chorus (reconstructed Hooke)

1872   '*The Language of Flowers*': song (Percival) (unpublished)
Chantant for piano

1873   *Credo* on themes from Beethoven symphonies for chorus and organ

1876   *Salve regina* for chorus and organ
Tantum ergo for chorus and organ

1877   *Reminiscences* for violin and piano
Peckham March for wind quintet
Study for strengthening the third finger for violin (re-copied and dedicated to Heifetz, 1920)

1878   *Fantasia* for violin and piano (unfinished)
String Quartets in D minor, B flat and A minor (all unfinished)
String Trio in C (unfinished)
Trio for two violins and piano (unfinished)
Six *Promenades* for wind quintet
Harmony Music Nos.1–4 for wind quintet
Andante con variazioni ('*Evesham andante*') for wind quintet
Adagio cantabile ('*Mrs Winslow's Soothing Syrup*')
Romance for violin and piano, Op.1
Allegro for oboe quartet (unfinished)

1878   *Menuetto* (scherzo) for orchestra (re-copied 1930)
(cont.)   *Symphony in G minor* after Mozart's *Symphony No.40*
         (part of first movement extant)
         Introductory Overture for the Christy Minstrels (lost)
         '*If she love me*': song (*Temple Bar Rondeau*)
            (unpublished)
         Hymn tunes in C, G and F major (the last quoted in
            Nursery Suite, 1931)
1879   *Domine, salvam fac reginam* for chorus and organ
         Tantum ergo for chorus and organ
         '*Brother, for thee He died*' for chorus and organ
         Fantasia on Irish Airs for violin and piano (unfinished)
         Two Polonaises for violin and piano (unfinished)
         Five Intermezzos for wind quintet
         Four Dances for wind quintet
         Harmony Music Nos.5 & 6 for wind quintet (*Andante
            arioso* from No.6 arranged as *Cantique* for small
            orchestra, Op.3, in 1912)
1879–84 Dances for Worcester City and County Pauper
         Lunatic Asylum, Powick (mostly quadrilles;
         No.5 of *L'Assommoir* used for *The Wand of Youth
         Suite* No.2, 1907)
c.1880s *Etudes caractéristiques pour violon seul* (published 1892)
1880   *String Quartet* fragments in E minor and A minor
1880   *O salutaris hostia* in F for chorus and organ
1881   *Harmony Music* No.7 for wind quintet
         Air de ballet (unpublished)
         Pas redoublé, Marches Nos.1 & 2
1882   *Air de ballet* (unpublished)
         Menuetto and Trio for piano trio; trio transcribed as
            Douce pensée for piano and scored for small
            orchestra (as *Rosemary*) in 1915
         Benedictus sit Deus pater for chorus, organ and strings
            (unfinished)
         O salutaris hostia in A for bass solo
1882–84 *Suite in D* for small orchestra; first three numbers
         revised as *Three Characteristic Pieces*, Op.10 (1899)
1883   *Fugue in D minor* for oboe and violin (unfinished)
1884   *Sevillana* for small orchestra, Op.7
         Une Idylle for violin and piano, Op.4 No.1

1884	*Pastourelle* for violin and piano, Op.4 No.2
(cont.)	*Griffinesque* for piano
	'A Soldier's Song' (C.F. Havell) (reissued in 1903 as 'A War Song')
1885	*Gavotte* for violin and piano
	Allegretto on GEDGE for violin and piano
	Overture, The Lakes (unfinished; lost)
	Scottish Overture (unfinished; lost)
	'Through the Long Days': song, Op.16 No.2 (J. Hay)
1886	*Piano Trio in D minor* (unfinished)
	Four Litanies for the Blessed Virgin Mary for unaccompanied chorus
	'Is she not Passing Fair?': song (Duc d'Orléans, translated by L. Costello)
1887	*Sonata* for violin and piano, Op.9 (destroyed; material included in *Sursum corda*, (Op.11)
	String Quartet, Op.8 (destroyed)
	Ave verum corpus for chorus and organ, Op.2 No.1 (originally set as *Pie Jesu*)
	Ave Maria for chorus and organ, Op.2 No.2
	Ave maris stella for chorus and organ, Op.2 No.3
	'A Song of Autumn': song (A. L. Gordon)
	'As I Laye a-thynkynge': song ('Thomas Ingoldsby')
	'Roundel': song (Swinburne) (unpublished)
1888	*String Quartet in D minor* (unfinished; *Intermezzo* completed as No.3 of *Vesper Voluntaries*, Op.14)
	Three pieces for string orchestra (lost, probably revised for *Serenade*, Op.20)
	Salut d'amour (*Liebesgrüss*) for violin and piano, Op.12 (also version for piano solo; orchestrated 1889)
	Ecce sacerdos magnus for chorus, organ and orchestra
	'The Wind at Dawn': song (C.A. Roberts) (orchestrated 1912)
1889	*Mot d'amour* (*Liebesahnung*) for violin and piano, Op.13 No.1
	Bizarrerie for violin and piano, Op.13 No.2
	Eleven Vesper Voluntaries for organ, Op.14
	Sonatina for piano (revised in 1931 for publication the following year)
	Presto for piano

1889   *'O Happy Eyes'*: partsong, Op.18 No.1 (C.A. Elgar)
(cont.)   *'My Love Dwelt in a Northern Land'*: partsong (A. Lang)
         'Queen Mary's Song' (Tennyson)
1889–92 *The Black Knight* for chorus and orchestra, Op.25
            (Uhland, translated by Longfellow)
1890   *Violin Concerto* (destroyed)
         Concert Overture, *Froissart*, Op.19
         Virelai for violin and piano, Op.4 No.3
1891   *La capricieuse* for violin and piano, Op.17
         'Spanish Serenade' (*'Stars of the Summer Night'*):
            accompanied partsong, Op.23 (Longfellow)
1892   *Serenade in E minor* for string orchestra, Op.20
         Very Melodious Exercises in the First Position for violin and
            piano, Op.22
         'Like to the Damask Rose': song (S. Wastell)
         'The Poet's Life': song (E. Burroughs)
         'The Shepherd's Song', Op.16 No.1 (B. Pain)
         'A Spear, a Sword': song
         'A Song of Autumn' (A.L. Gordon)
1893   *Offertoire* (*Andante religioso*) for violin and piano
1894   *Sursum corda* for strings, brass, organ and timpani,
            Op.11
         'The Snow': accompanied partsong, Op.26 No.1
            (C.A. Elgar)
         'Fly, Singing Bird': accompanied partsong, Op.26 No.2
            (C.A. Elgar)
         'Rondel': song, Op.16 No.3 (Froissart, translated by
            Longfellow)
         'The Wave': song
         'The Muleteer's Song'
1895   *Sonata in G* (No.1) for organ, Op.28
         Scenes from the Bavarian Highlands for chorus and
            orchestra (or piano) (C.A. Elgar, after Bavarian
            folksongs)
         'After': song, Op.31 No.1 (P.B. Marston)
         'A Song of Flight': song, Op.31 No.2 (C. Rossetti)
1894–96 *Scenes from the Saga of King Olaf*: cantata, Op.30
            (Longfellow and H.A. Acworth)
1895–96 *The Light of Life* (*Lux Christi*): short oratorio, Op.29
            (E. Capel-Cure, based on the Bible)

1896–97   *The Banner of St George*: ballad for chorus and
orchestra, Op.33

1897   *Te Deum and Benedictus* for chorus and organ or
orchestra, Op.34

Minuet for piano or small orchestra, Op.21

Chanson de nuit for violin and piano, Op.15 No.1
(arranged for small orchestra 1899)

Imperial March for orchestra, Op.32

Lute Song, 'Love Alone Will Stay' (C.A. Elgar) (revised
as No.2 of *Sea Pictures*, Op.37)

1897–99   *Chanson de matin* for violin and piano, Op.15 No.2
(arranged for small orchestra 1899)

1898   *Caractacus*: cantata, Op.35 (Acworth)

Festive March in C for orchestra (only fragment
survives)

O salutaris hostia in E flat for chorus and organ

1898–99   *Variations on an Original Theme* ('*Enigma*'), Op.36

1899   *Sea Pictures* for contralto or mezzo-soprano and
orchestra, Op.37

Sérénade Lyrique for small orchestra

'*To her beneath whose Steadfast Star*': partsong
(F.W.H. Myers) '*Dry those Fair, those Crystal Eyes*':
song (H. King)

1900   *The Dream of Gerontius*, Op.38 (Newman)

'*The Pipes of Pan*': song (A. Ross)

1901   *Pomp and Circumstance Marches* Nos.1 in D major (see
also *Coronation Ode*) and 2 in A minor, Op.39

Concert Overture, *Cockaigne* (*In London Town*), Op.40

Incidental music, Funeral March and *Song* ('*There are
seven that pull the thread*') to *Grania and Diarmid*
(play by Moore, song lyrics by W.B. Yeats)

May Song for piano or violin and piano (orchestrated
1928)

Skizze for piano

Concert Allegro for piano, Op.46 (revised 1906)

'*Come, Gentle Night*': song (C. Bingham)

'*Always and Everywhere*': song (Krasinski, translated by
F.E. Fortey)

1902   *Coronation Ode*, Op.44 (Benson) (the finale, '*Land of
Hope and Glory*', uses the trio melody of *Pomp and*

List of Works

1902 (cont.)	*Circumstance March* No.1 and was also arranged as a song) *Dream Children*, two pieces for small orchestra (or piano) after Lamb, Op.43 *Five Partsongs from the Greek Anthology* for male voices, Op.45 '*Weary Wind of the West*': partsong (T.E. Brown) '*In the Dawn*' and '*Speak, Music*': songs, Op.41 Nos.1 & 2 (A.C. Benson)
1902–3	*The Apostles*: oratorio, Op.49 (Elgar, based on the Bible)
1903–4	Concert Overture, *In the South* (*Alassio*), Op.50 (section titled '*Canto Popolare*' – Elgar's own invention – available separately for small orchestra and various instrumental combinations)
1903–6	*The Kingdom:* oratorio, Op.51 (Elgar, based on the Bible and the Didache)
1904	*Pomp and Circumstance March* No.3 in C minor, Op.39
1904–5	*Introduction and Allegro* for string quartet and string orchestra, Op.47 (first sketches 1901)
1905	*In Smyrna* for piano '*Evening Scene*': partsong (Patmore)
1906	*For Dot's Nuns* for organ (his sister Dot was in a convent)
1907	*The Wand of Youth Suites* Nos.1 & 2, Opp.1a & 1b (incorporating earliest tunes – see also first entry and *The Starlight Express*, Op.78) *Pomp and Circumstance March* No.4 in G major (see also *The King's Way*, 1909) *Andantino* for violin, mandolin and guitar (unfinished) *String Quartet* fragments (later used in *Symphony No.1* and *The Music Makers*) '*How Calmly the Evening*': partsong (T. Lynch) '*The Reveille*': partsong for male voices, Op.54 (Bret Harte) '*Love*': partsong, Op.18 No.2 (A. Maquarie) Four Choral Settings, Op.53: '*There is Sweet Music*' (Tennyson); '*Deep in my Soul*' (Byron); '*O Wild West Wind*' (Shelley); '*Owls*' (Elgar) '*A Christmas Greeting*' for voices, two violins and piano, Op.52 (C.A. Elgar)

1907 (cont.)	*'Marching Song'* (W. de Courcy Stretton) (reissued in 1914 as *'Follow the Colours'*)
1907–8	*Symphony No.1* in A flat, Op.55
1908	*'Pleading'*: song, Op.48 (A. L. Salmon) (also orchestrated)
1909	*Elegy* for string orchestra, Op.58

1909   Two single chants for the *Venite*

Two double chants for Psalms 68 & 75

'Lo! Christ the Lord is Born': carol for unaccompanied chorus (adapted from *Grete Malverne on a Rock*, sent as a Christmas card in 1897)

'Angelus (Tuscany)': partsong, Op.56 (words from Tuscan dialect)

'Go, Song of Mine': partsong, Op.57 (Cavalcanti, translated by D.G. Rossetti)

Elegy, *'They are at Rest'*: partsong (Newman)

'A Child Asleep': song (E.B. Browning)

'The King's Way': song (C.A. Elgar) (uses the trio melody of *Pomp and Circumstance March* No.4)

'The Torch': song (Elgar as 'Pietro d'Alba') (orchestrated 1912)

1909–10   *Song-cycle with orchestra*, Op.59 Nos.3, 5 & 6 (Gilbert Parker) (1, 2 & 4 never composed)

Violin Concerto in B minor, Op.61

1909–11   *Symphony No.2* in E flat major, Op.63 (first sketches 1903)

1910   *Romance* for bassoon and orchestra, Op.62

'The River': song (Elgar as 'Pietro d'Alba') (orchestrated 1912)

1910–12   *'Great is the Lord'* (Psalm 48): anthem for chorus and organ or orchestra, Op.67

1911   *Coronation March*, Op.65 (incorporating parts of 1902 Rabelais ballet)

'O Hearken Thou' (from Psalm 5): anthem for chorus and organ or orchestra, Op.64

1912   *The Music Makers*: ode, Op.69 (O'Shaughnessy) (including quotations from earlier works)

The Crown of India: masque, Op.66 (incorporating sketches from 1902 onwards and part of *In Smyrna*)

1913   *Carissima* for small orchestra
        Falstaff: symphonic study in C minor with two
          interludes in A minor, Op.68

1914   *Sospiri* for strings, harp and organ, Op.70
        Carillon: recitation with orchestra, Op.75
          (Cammaerts)
        '*Give unto the Lord*' (Psalm 29): anthem for chorus
          and organ or orchestra, Op.74
        '*Fear not, O Land*' (from *Joel II*): harvest anthem for
          chorus and organ
        Two Choral Songs for unaccompanied chorus, Op.71:
          '*The Shower*' and '*The Fountain*' (Vaughan)
        Choral Song, '*Death on the Hills*' for unaccompanied
          chorus, Op.72 (Maikov, translated by Newmarch)
        Two Choral Songs for unaccompanied chorus, Op.73:
          '*Love's Tempest*' (Maikov, translated by Newmarch)
          and '*Serenade*' (Minsky, translated by Newmarch)
        '*The Birthright*': unison song with bugles and drums
          (G.A. Stocks)
        '*Arabian Serenade*': song (M. Lawrence)
        '*The Chariots of the Lord*': song (J. Brownlie)
        '*Soldier's Song*' (H. Begbie) (unpublished and
          suppressed)

1915   Incidental music for *The Starlight Express*, Op.78 (play
          by V. Pearn after Blackwood) (incorporating
          themes from *The Wand of Youth*; three of the *Organ
          Grinder's Songs* published separately in 1916)
        Polonia: symphonic prelude, Op.76
        '*Une voix dans le désert*': recitation and song with
          orchestra, Op.77 (Cammaerts)

1915–17 *The Spirit of England*, Op.80 (Binyon)

1916   '*Fight for Right*': song (W. Morris)

1917   *The Sanguine Fan*: ballet, Op.81
        '*Le drapeau belge*': recitation with orchestra
          (Cammaerts)
        '*The Fringes of the Fleet*': songs for four baritones and
          orchestra (Kipling) (with later addition of song
          for baritones unaccompanied to text of Gilbert
          Parker)
        '*Ozymandias*': song (Shelley)

1918	*Violin Sonata* in E minor, Op.82
	String Quartet in E minor, Op.83
	'*Big Steamers*': song (Kipling)
1918–19	*Piano Quintet* in A minor, Op.84
	Cello Concerto in E minor, Op.85
1922	'*The Ballad of Brave Hector*' and '*The Worcestershire Squire*': songs with unison chorus (E. Anderson) (unfinished)
1923	Incidental music to *King Arthur* (play by Binyon)
	Memorial Chime for Loughborough War Memorial Carillon (unpublished)
	'*The Wanderer*': partsong (anon., adapted by Elgar)
	'*Zut! Zut! Zut!* ': partsong (Elgar as 'Richard Mardon')
1924	*Empire March* (also arranged in an unpublished version for piano trio)
	Songs and a partsong from *Pageant of Empire* (A. Noyes)
	'*The Bull (in May Week)*': unison song for male voice and optional chorus (F. Hamilton)
1925	'*The Herald* ': partsong for male voices (A. Smith)
	'*The Prince of Sleep*': partsong (de la Mare)
1927	*Civic Fanfare* for the opening of the Hereford Festival (unpublished)
1928	Incidental music to *Beau Brummel* (play by B. Matthews) (only *Minuet* published)
	'*I Sing the Birth*': carol for unaccompanied chorus (Jonson)
1929	'*Goodmorrow*': carol for unaccompanied chorus based on an early hymn tune (G. Gascoigne)
1929–33	*The Spanish Lady*: opera, Op.89 (after Ben Jonson's *The Devil is an Ass*) (unfinished, incorporating sketches of a lifetime. Critical edition edited by Percy Young)
1930	*Severn Suite* for brass band, Op.87 (based on early sketches and arranged for orchestra in 1932)
	Pomp and Circumstance March No.5 in C major, Op.39
	Soliloquy for oboe (orchestrated by Gordon Jacob, 1967)
	'*It isnae me*': song (S. Holmes)
1931	*Nursery Suite* for small orchestra
1932	*So Many True Princesses*: ode for chorus and military band
	Serenade for piano

1932   *Adieu* for piano
(cont.) '*The Rapid Stream*', '*The Woodland Stream*' and '*When
         Swallows Fly*': unison children's choruses (Mackay)
1932–33 *Symphony No.3* in C minor (unfinished)
1933   *Mina* for small orchestra
        Organ Sonata No.2 in B flat, Op.87a (arrangement by
         Ivor Atkins of the *Severn Suite)*

MAJOR ARRANGEMENTS, ORCHESTRATIONS AND TRANSCRIPTIONS OF WORKS BY OTHER COMPOSERS

1880(?) Schumann: *Scherzo* from *Overture, Scherzo and Finale*,
         Op.52 (unpublished)
1883   Wagner: *Entry of the Minstrels* from *Tannhäuser*
         (unpublished)
1894   Wagner: *Good Friday Music* from *Parsifal* –
         arrangement for small orchestra (unpublished)
1901   Brewer: *Emmaus*
1902   *God Save the King* for soprano, chorus and orchestra
1911   Bach: Two Chorales from the *St Matthew Passion* for
         brass (unpublished)
1921–22 Bach: *Fantasia and Fugue in C minor*, BWV537
1922   Parry: *Jerusalem*
1923   Handel: *Overture in D minor* from *Chandos Anthem* No.2
        Battishill: '*O Lord, Look down from Heaven*'
        Wesley: '*Let us Lift up our Hearts*'
1929   Purcell: '*Jehova, quam multi sunt hostes mei* '
1933   Chopin: *Funeral March* from *Piano Sonata* (No.2) in
         B flat minor

EDWARD ELGAR: RECOMMENDED RECORDINGS

(1) THE COMPOSER AS CONDUCTOR

All the recordings Elgar conducted or supervised, from *Carissima* in January 1914 to the *Caractacus* excerpts he guided from his sickbed in January 1934, are covered by two record companies and amount to an astonishing fourteen CDs.

Pearl's five-CD set (GEMM CDS 9951–5) features the pre-electrical recordings, necessarily compromised by the number of musicians that could be used and with cuts in the larger-scale works; there are, nevertheless, some pieces of vital interest that Elgar did not re-record.

Each of EMI's three sets, with three CDs apiece, contains essential interpretations which, in the view of many, have never been surpassed. Volume One (CDS 7 54560 2) includes the two symphonies, *Falstaff*, and an outstanding account of the Prelude to *The Dream of Gerontius* recorded live in the Royal Albert Hall. Volume Two (CDS 7 54564 2) begins with a volatile '*Enigma*' *Variations*, and the *Violin Concerto* with the fifteen-year-old Yehudi Menuhin. Volume Three (CDS 7 54568 2) boasts the most invigorating performance of the Overture *In the South* ever committed to disc, and Beatrice Harrison in the *Cello Concerto*.

The concertos are available separately on a single disc (EMI CDC 5 55221 2), and the '*Enigma*' *Variations* are coupled with Holst's ragged performance of *The Planets* on EMI CDC 7 54837 2.

(2) RECOMMENDED RECORDINGS OF THE STEREO ERA

Where the performance chosen is coupled with another that may not be the top recommendation, the accompanying work is prefixed by 'c/w' and only the artist(s) of the recommended recording given.

Orchestral

Carillon (orchestral part only); Dream Children;
Grania and Diarmid – Incidental Music and Funeral
March; Polonia; Elegy; Caractacus – March; Imperial
March; Coronation March (c/w marches by Walton)
♦ LPO / Boult ⊗ EMI CDM 5 65584 2

Cello Concerto*; Sea Pictures**
♦ *du Pré / **Baker / LSO / Barbirolli ⊗ EMI CDC 7 47329 2

'Enigma' Variations; Overtures, Cockaigne and
Froissart
♦ LPO / Slatkin ⊗ RCA 09026 60073 2

Falstaff (c/w 'Enigma' Variations*)
♦ Hallé Orchestra / *Philharmonia / Barbirolli
⊗ EMI CDM 7 69185 2

Overture, In the South (c/w Symphony No.2)
♦ LPO / Solti ⊗ Decca 430 150-2DSP

Introduction and Allegro for strings; Serenade for
strings; Elegy*; Sospiri* (c/w Vaughan Williams: Fantasia on
a theme by Thomas Tallis; Fantasia on 'Greensleeves')
♦ Sinfonia of London / *New Philharmonia / Barbirolli
⊗ EMI CDC 7 47537 2

'The Lighter Elgar': Romance for bassoon and
orchestra; Three Characteristic Pieces; Minuet;
May Song; Sevillana; Rosemary; Sérénade lyrique;
Carissima; Mina; Chanson de matin*; Minuet from
Beau Brummel*; Two Songs from The Starlight
Express*; Sun Dance from The Wand of Youth
Suite No.1*; Dream Children*; Salut d'amour*
♦ Northern Sinfonia / Marriner, *Harvey / RPO /
Collingwood ⊗ EMI CDM 5 65593 2

Nursery Suite (c/w The Wand of Youth Suites Nos.1 & 2)
♦ Ulster Orchestra / Thomson ⊗ Chandos CHAN 8318

Pomp and Circumstance Marches Nos.1–5 (c/w Overtures, Cockaigne and Froissart)
♦ Philharmonia / New Philharmonia / Barbirolli
⊗ EMI CDM 7 69563 2

Severn Suite: original version scored by Henry Geehl for brass band (c/w music for brass by Foster, Hogarth Lear, Holst, Howarth and Sousa)
♦ Grimethorpe Colliery Band / Howarth
⊗ Belart 450 023–2

Symphony No.1 (c/w Cockaigne Overture)
♦ Philharmonia / Barbirolli
⊗ EMI CDM 7 64511 2

Symphony No.2 (c/w Cockaigne Overture)
♦ LPO / Boult ⊗ EMI CDM 7 64014 2

Symphony No.3 – sketches (see under STAGE WORKS: The Spanish Lady)

Violin Concerto
♦ Kennedy / LPO / Handley ⊗ EMI Eminence CD-EMX 2058

The Wand of Youth Suites Nos.1 & 2; Songs from The Starlight Express; Dream Children
♦ Hagley / Terfel / WNO Orchestra / Mackerras
⊗ Argo 433 214-2

Vocal and choral

The Apostles
♦ Hargan / Hodgson / Rendall / Terfel / Roberts / Lloyd / LSC / LSO / Hickox ⊗ Chandos CHAN 8875 / 6 (2 CDs)

The Banner of St George; Great is the Lord (Psalm 48); Te Deum and Benedictus
♦ LSC / Northern Sinfonia / Hickox
⊗ EMI CDM 5 65108 2

The Black Knight; Scenes from the Saga of King Olaf*
(c/w 'Spanish Serenade', 'The Snow' and 'Fly, Singing Bird')
♦ Liverpool PC / RLPO / Groves, *Cahill / Langridge /
  Rayner Cook / LPC / LPO / Handley
  ⊗ EMI CMS 5 65104 2 (2 CDs)

Caractacus; Severn Suite (version for orchestra)
♦ Howarth / Davies / Wilson-Johnson / Roberts / Miles / LSC
  / LSO / Hickox ⊗ Chandos CHAN 9156 / 7 (2 CDs)

Cathedral and church music: Ave verum corpus; Ave Maria; Ave maris stella; Angelus; I Sing the Birth; Lo! Christ the Lord is born; Great is the Lord; Ecce sacerdos magnus; O salutaris hostia Nos.1–3; Fear not, O Land; O Hearken Thou (Coronation Anthem for George V); Give unto the Lord
♦ Partington / Worcester Cathedral Choir / Hunt
  ⊗ Hyperion CDA66313

The Dream of Gerontius; Sea Pictures*
♦ Baker / Lewis / Borg / Sheffield PC / Ambrosian Singers /
  Hallé Chorus and Orchestra / *LSO / Barbirolli
  ⊗ EMI CMS 7 63185 2 (2 CDs)

The Kingdom; Coronation Ode*
♦ Price / Minton / Young / Shirley-Quirk / LPC / LPO /
  Boult, *Lott / Hodgson / Morton / Roberts / CUMS /
  Choir of King's College Cambridge / New Philharmonia /
  Kneller Hall Band / Ledger
  ⊗ EMI CMS 7 64209 2 (2 CDs)

The Light of Life
♦ Howarth / Finnie / Davies / Shirley-Quirk / LSC / LSO /
  Hickox ⊗ Chandos CHAN 9208

The Music Makers
(Sir Adrian Boult's incandescent recording with Janet Baker
  was unavailable at the time of writing. The version listed
  below is an interim recommendation.)
♦ Rigby / BBCSO / Davis ⊗ Teldec 4509-92374-2

Partsongs: Three Partsongs, Op.18; Five Partsongs from the Greek Anthology; Four Partsongs, Op.53; Two Partsongs, Op.71; 'Death on the Hills'; Two Partsongs, Op.73; 'How Calmly the Evening'; 'Weary Wind of the West'; 'Evening Scene'; 'The Prince of Sleep'; 'Go, Song of Mine'

♦ Finzi Singers / Spicer ⊗ Chandos CHAN 9269
♦ A less distinguished, but complete, survey of the choral songs from the Worcester Cathedral Choir and the Donald Hunt Singers is also available
⊗ Hyperion CDA66271 / 2 (2 CDs)

Scenes from the Bavarian Highlands (c/w The Black Knight)
♦ LSC / LSO / Hickox ⊗ Chandos CHAN 9436

Songs for voice and orchestra: 'Pleading'; Three Songs, Op.59; Two Songs, Op.60 (c/w songs by Vaughan Williams and Butterworth)
♦ Tear / CBSO / Handley ⊗ EMI CDM 7 64731 2

The Spirit of England (c/w Coronation Ode)
♦ Cahill / SNO / Gibson ⊗ Chandos CHAN 6574

Stage works

Crown of India Suite (c/w Symphony No.2)
♦ SNO / Gibson ⊗ Chandos CHAN 6523

King Arthur Suite (c/w excerpts from The Starlight Express)
♦ Bournemouth Sinfonietta / Hurst ⊗ Chandos CHAN 6582

The Spanish Lady – unfinished opera edited by Percy Young; **sketches for the Third Symphony*** in a talk presented by Anthony Payne
♦ Veira / Maltman / Cannan / Morris / Storey / Ewing / Milne / Scottish Opera Ch / BBCSSO / Manson, *BBCPO / Tortelier
⊗ BBC MM138 (disc available only with Vol.IV No.2 of the *BBC Music Magazine*)

The Starlight Express – incidental music
♦ Masterson / Hammond-Stroud / LPO / Handley
⊗ EMI Eminence CD EMX 2267

Chamber

Music for wind quintet – Volume One: Harmony Music Nos.1 & 5; Five Intermezzos; Adagio cantabile ('Mrs Winslow's Soothing Syrup'); Andante con variazione ('Evesham Andante')
♦ Athena Ensemble ⊗ Chandos CHAN 6553

Music for wind quintet – Volume Two: Harmony Music Nos.2–4; Six Promenades; Four Dances
♦ Athena Ensemble ⊗ Chandos CHAN 6554

Piano Quintet; String Quartet
♦ Roberts / Chilingirian String Quartet ⊗ EMI CDM 5 65099 2

Violin Sonata; Salut d'amour*; Mot d'amour; Chanson de nuit; Chanson de matin; Canto popolare; six very easy pieces in the first position
♦ Kennedy / *Isserlis / Pettinger ⊗ Chandos CHAN 8380

Instrumental

Organ Sonata No.1; Vesper Voluntaries – Introduction and Andante (c/w church and cathedral music)
♦ Sumsion ⊗ EMI CDM 5 65594 2

Piano music: Concert Allegro; In Smyrna; Chantant; Pastourelle; Rosemary; Griffinesque, Sonatine (1889 and 1931 versions); Presto; Minuet; May Song; Dream Children; Skizze; Carissima; Serenade; Adieu
♦ Pettinger ⊗ Chandos CHAN 8438

SELECTED
FURTHER READING

The following list includes works most frequently quoted, with special indebtedness to Jerrold Northrop Moore's scrupulously edited volume of Elgar letters. Readers seeking a more thorough chronicle of events in Elgar's life, year by year, are referred to Northrop Moore's exhaustive biography.

Robert Anderson, *Elgar in Manuscript* (The British Library, 1990)

Rosa Burley and F.C. Carruthers, *Elgar: the Record of a Friendship* (Barrie & Jenkins, 1972)

Michael Kennedy, *Portrait of Elgar* (Oxford University Press, 1968; revised edition 1973)

Basil Maine, *Elgar: his Life and Works* (G. Bell 1933; reprinted by Cedric Chivers Ltd)

Jerrold Northrop Moore, *Edward Elgar: a Creative Life* (Oxford University Press, 1984)

Jerrold Northrop Moore (editor), *Edward Elgar: Letters of a Lifetime* (Oxford University Press, 1990)

Jerrold Northrop Moore (editor), *Elgar and his Publishers: Letters of a Creative Life* (Oxford University Press, two volumes, 1987)

W.H. Reed, *Elgar as I knew him* (Gollancz, 1936; revised edition 1973)

W.H. Reed, *Elgar* (Dent Master Musicians, 1939)

Percy M. Young (editor), *Letters to Nimrod* (Dennis Dobson, 1965)

Index

THE
CLASSIC *f*M
GUIDE TO
CLASSICAL MUSIC

JEREMY NICHOLAS

*' . . . a fascinating and accessible guide . . . it will provide
an informative and illuminating source of insight
for everybody from the beginner to the musicologist.'*

Sir Edward Heath

The Classic fM Guide to Classical Music opens with a masterly
history of classical music, illustrated with charts and lifelines, and
is followed by a comprehensive guide to more than 500 composers. There are major entries detailing the lives and works of the
world's most celebrated composers, as well as concise biographies
of more than 300 others.

This invaluable companion to classical music combines extensive
factual detail with fascinating anecdotes, and an insight into the
historical and musical influences of the great composers. It also
contains reviews and recommendations of the best works, and
extensive cross-references to lesser-known composers. Jeremy
Nicholas's vibrant, informative and carefully researched text is
complemented by photographs and cartoons, and is designed for
easy reference, with a comprehensive index.

£19.99   ISBN: **1 85793 760 0**   **Hardback**
£9.99   ISBN: **1 86205 051 1**   **Paperback**

CLASSIC *f*M
COMPACT COMPANIONS

CHOPIN, PUCCINI, ROSSINI, TCHAIKOVSKY

In association with *Classic fM* and *Philips Classics*, this revolutionary new series, *Compact Companions*, is a stylish package of book and compact disc. Each title provides the ultimate prelude to the lives and works of the most popular composers of classical music.

These composers' extraordinary, eventful lives and their powerful, moving music make them the ideal subjects for combined reading and listening. Written by respected authors, the texts provide a comprehensive introduction to the life and work of the composer, and each includes a richly illustrated biography, a complete list of works and a definitive list of recommended recordings. The accompanying CD combines both favourite and less-well-known pieces, recorded by artists of world renown.

Chopin
Christopher Headington
ISBN: 1 85793 655 8

Puccini
Jonathon Brown
ISBN: 1 85793 660 4

Rossini
David Mountfield
ISBN: 1 85793 665 5

Tchaikovsky
David Nice
ISBN: 1 85793 670 1

£9.99 (inc. VAT) each companion

These books can be ordered direct from the publisher.
Please contact the Marketing Department.
But try your bookshop first.

CLASSIC *f*M
LIFELINES

With 4.8 million listeners every week, *Classic fM* is now the most listened-to national commercial radio station in the UK. With the launch of **Classic fM Lifelines**, Pavilion Books and *Classic fM* are creating an affordable series of elegantly designed short biographies that will put everyone's favourite composers into focus.

Written with enthusiasm and in a highly accessible style, the **Classic fM Lifelines** series will become the Everyman of musical biographies. Titles for the series have been chosen from *Classic fM*'s own listener surveys of the most popular composers.

TITLES PUBLISHED:

Johannes Brahms
Jonathon Brown
ISBN: 1 85793 967 0

Claude Debussy
Jonathon Brown
ISBN: 1 85793 972 7

Edward Elgar
David Nice
ISBN: 1 85793 977 8

Gustav Mahler
Julian Haylock
ISBN: 1 85793 982 4

Sergei Rachmaninov
Julian Haylock
ISBN: 1 85793 944 1

Franz Schubert
Stephen Jackson
ISBN: 1 85793 987 5

£4.99 each book

FORTHCOMING TITLES:

- ♦ *J.S. Bach*
- ♦ *Ludwig van Beethoven*
- ♦ *Benjamin Britten*

- ♦ *Joseph Haydn*
- ♦ *Dmitri Shostakovich*
- ♦ *Ralph Vaughan Williams*

CLASSIC *f*M
LIFELINES

To purchase any of the books in the *Classic fM Lifelines* series
simply fill in the order form below and post or fax it,
together with your remittance, to the address below.

Please send the titles ticked below
(*published spring 1997)

Johannes Brahms	☐	*J.S. Bach	☐
Claude Debussy	☐	*Ludwig van Beethoven	☐
Edward Elgar	☐	*Benjamin Britten	☐
Gustav Mahler	☐	*Joseph Haydn	☐
Sergei Rachmaninov	☐	*Dmitri Shostakovich	☐
Franz Schubert	☐	*Ralph Vaughan Williams	☐

Number of titles @ £4.99 _____   Value: £_____

Add 10% of total value for postage and packing   Value: £_____

Total value of order: £_____

I enclose a cheque (UK only) payable to Pavilion Books Ltd ☐

OR

Please charge my credit card account ☐

I wish to pay by: Visa ☐ MasterCard ☐ Access ☐ American Express ☐

Card number ☐☐☐☐☐☐☐☐☐☐☐☐☐☐☐☐☐☐

Signature_____   Expiry Date_____

Name _____

Address _____

_____

_____   Postcode_____

Please send your order to: Marketing Department, Pavilion Books Ltd,
26 Upper Ground, London SE1 9PD, or fax for quick dispatch to:
Marketing Department, 0171-620 0042.